"*Beirut to Boston* is a mouth-watering romp through the culinary legacy of two different cultures, told through the eyes and recipes of one of Boston's best chefs, a great friend and my globetrotting partner in cooking, Jay Hajj."

—KEN ORINGER,
James Beard Award–winning chef

"Jay Hajj is one of the best chefs I've ever met. Readers will love learning the secrets to everything from Lebanese street-food favorites like manakish to the turkey dishes that made Mike's City Diner in Boston one of America's most beloved eateries."

—JAMIE BISSONNETTE,
James Beard Award–winning chef

"Tommy would be so proud and honored to be a part of this book. [It is] truly a unique perspective on our time-honored tradition of hope and freedom for a better life, all while traveling through Jay's life journey of food and culture to his American dream."

—ANGELA MENINO,
former first lady of Boston
and wife to the late mayor of Boston, Thomas M. Menino

"Jay Hajj is inspiring. He epitomizes the American Dream. His food shows us the love he has for America, for Boston and for his Lebanese culture. Through this book the world can get to meet Jay. He's the real deal."

—BOB KRAMER,
master bladesmith and founder of Kramer Knives

"From battle-scarred Beirut to Boston's best breakfast and brunch, Jay's story is both inspiring and delicious."

—MAT SCHAFFER,
Boston restaurant critic

Beirut to Boston
A COOKBOOK

COMFORT FOOD
INSPIRED BY
A RAGS-TO-RESTAURANTS
STORY

JAY HAJJ
CHEF AND OWNER OF MIKE'S CITY DINER
WINNER OF *GUY'S GROCERY GAMES* AND FEATURED ON FOOD NETWORK'S *DINERS, DRIVE-INS, AND DIVES*

WITH KERRY J. BYRNE
WRITER FOR THE *BOSTON HERALD*

PAGE STREET
PUBLISHING CO.

PAGE STREET
PUBLISHING CO.

First published in 2017 by

Page Street Publishing Co.

27 Congress Street, Suite 105

Salem, MA 01970

www.pagestreetpublishing.com

Distributed by Macmillan, sales in Canada by The Canadian Manda Group.

21   20   19   18   17   1   2   3   4   5

ISBN-13: 978-1-62414-342-7

ISBN-10: 1-62414-342-3

Library of Congress Control Number: 2016917976

Cover and book design by Page Street Publishing Co.

Photography by Ken Goodman

Written with Kerry J. Byrne

Printed and bound in the United States

 As a member of 1% for the Planet, Page Street Publishing protects our planet by donating to nonprofits like The Trustees, which focuses on local land conservation. Learn more at onepercentfortheplanet.org.

Dedicated to my father and mother, Nicolas and Samira Hajj.
They left behind all they knew to give us a better life.

Contents

FOREWORD

When I think of Boston, like a lot of other people, I think of the Red Sox, the New England Patriots, the Boston Tea Party and a city rich in American history.

But to me, it's also city with a big-time food identity well beyond just "chowdah" and "lobstah." And my buddy Jay Hajj from Mike's City Diner is about the greatest representative of the Boston scene that I've come across. He may have been born in Beirut, but the Jay I know is a Bostonian to the bone.

I first met Jay when I was in Boston shooting *Diners, Drive-Ins, and Dives* and I knew right away that he was the real deal. He's a hard-working, self-made restaurateur who makes you just want to get in the kitchen and cook with him. Since we first met on DDD, we've cooked together a million times. From Food Network's *Guy's Big Bite* where Jay did his version of New England clam chowder to competing on *Guy's Grocery Games* to cookin' it up at my birthday bash, Jay and I have seen some serious kitchen action together and most importantly, we've become brothers.

And not only can he cook, he's got a huge heart and he shares it generously with his guests and his city. Jay was one of the first chefs to jump in with me on our annual Cooking With Best Buddies Food & Wine Festival where along with founder Anthony Shriver and Patriots great Tom Brady, we work to raise awareness and money for Best Buddies International, an amazing organization dedicated to helping people with intellectual and developmental disabilities.

But just being a good guy doesn't mean you should have a restaurant or write a cookbook. And that's where Mike's City Diner and Jay's truly unique background come in. You're not gonna find anyone who doesn't dig Mike's City Diner's Famous Pilgrim Sandwich—everything you've ever loved about Thanksgiving all rolled into one big-time sandwich—or his famous hash.

But it's not just all diner classics here, you'll also find an incredible global array of foods, representing the various cultural influences that have inspired Jay's cooking. The homemade chicken liver pâté with pomegranate, onion and bacon marmalade is inspired by a dish Jay ate while escaping the war zone of Beirut in the 1970s. All the different recipes for *manakish*, a kind of Lebanese pizza, are amazing. And the chicken with 50 cloves of garlic . . . my mouth is watering right now even talking about it.

In this book, you even get some behind-the-scenes recipes from the late, great Locke-Ober, Boston's most famous restaurant for more than 100 years. Today it's called Yvonne's, and Jay is one of the partners behind it. We've shared some amazing food at this beautiful restaurant and, yes, this book shares some of Yvonne's recipes too.

Jay Hajj is a true character with an inspiring story and an uncanny ability to tell that story through food. This book is that very story and I know you'll dig it as much as I do.

Guy!

INTRODUCTION

This book is a journey in many ways. It's an immigrant's journey, a uniquely American journey and a culinary journey —told through the food and recipes of my life as a chef, shaped by two very different cities on opposite sides of the world: beautiful but troubled Beirut, the Paris of the East, and smart but pugnacious Boston, the Athens of America.

This is, at its core, a book about the American Dream. And I'm happy to say the American Dream is alive and well. I know because I've lived it. And I've seen many friends, from all corners of the globe, live this dream too.

My journey began as a boy in war-torn Beirut, caught quite literally in the cross fire of the Lebanese Civil War. My father Nicolas provided for the family, but when the war came he was often away serving in the Lebanese army. My mom Samira had to care for her four children, and of course feed us under difficult circumstances. During the good times, we lived cramped in a small apartment in the middle of the city. Then the war exploded outside our fourth-floor window in 1975, during a violent incident still known ominously today as the Bus Massacre.

The foods we ate to survive were Lebanese versions of the time-honored cuisine of the Arab and Middle Eastern worlds. Beans. Rice. Lamb on occasion. Plenty of fresh and colorful fruits and vegetables such as figs, lemons and pomegranates. And the beautiful, aromatic spices of the Middle East and Mediterranean, including allspice, cinnamon and Aleppo pepper, all of which flavor the pages of this book.

The Middle Eastern comfort food of my childhood has since been complemented by the hearty, often oversized and globally influenced cuisine of my adopted homeland of the United States.

We moved to Boston when I was an 8-year-old boy and it instantly opened up a whole new world to me in many different ways. Food was central to that immigrant experience. I discovered Greek, Italian, Irish and Asian food. And plenty of fresh, beautiful New England seafood. Food and flavors I never knew existed when I lived in Lebanon. By age 13, I was cooking in local restaurants, learning to master this new world of food and flavor. Food was essential to my assimilation. It's how I discovered the amazing cultural patchwork that is the United States. Food is the path I followed to become an American.

Today, I own Mike's City Diner in Boston's South End, which I purchased back in 1996 and which has since been recognized as one of the best diners in the nation. The success of Mike's has afforded me an opportunity to invest in other signature restaurant properties around Boston.

Perhaps no dining concept is more uniquely American than the diner. And Mike's serves quintessentially American diner fare: hearty breakfasts of eggs, meat and potatoes, fluffy pancakes doused in syrup and, for lunch, Reubens, cheesesteaks and triple-decker clubs of ham, roast beef or turkey.

And, oh, the turkeys! We bake delicious turkeys every day. Those beautiful fresh-cooked turkeys put Mike's City Diner on the map. We serve turkey every way imaginable, from complete Thanksgiving dinners, to turkey hash, to turkey soup, to Mike's City Diner's Famous Pilgrim Sandwich, recognized by the Food Network as one of the Top 5 Thanksgiving dishes in America!

How cool is that? This immigrant kid from Lebanon made his name in America mastering the most iconic American meal: Thanksgiving dinner. It makes me very proud.

My story is much like that of countless immigrants who arrive on our shores each year and forge their own path to a better life. In my case, that path was flavored by the comfort-food cuisine of two different cities and two different cultures, then woven together in a uniquely American tapestry. This book chronicles the sights, aromas and flavors of that American story, of my American journey. I hope you enjoy the ride!

Jay Hajj

CHAPTER 1

Bill Clinton's Southern-Style Breakfast

Bill Clinton, the president of the United States, sat right across from me, eating smoked ham and eggs with grits and corn bread, chatting like we were old pals.

So many emotions ran through my head at that moment I can hardly explain it all these years later. I can still barely believe it happened. You see, when I was a boy in Lebanon during the Civil War, there was a lot of violence and death. My parents Nicolas and Samira knew they needed a better life for their children. They knew the United States was the most powerful and most welcoming country in the world. They knew the Land of Opportunity would offer us a shot at that better life. And so here I was 20 years later, fulfilling those dreams my parents had. I was the owner of my own business and, completely unexpectedly, was eating breakfast with the president of the country that my parents dreamed of back in Lebanon. Where else in the world could that happen to a poor kid from a war-torn country?

President Bill Clinton came from humble roots himself and he was a southern boy from Arkansas. It turns out he loved homestyle, full-flavored food. And Mike's City Diner was one of the few places in Boston he could find that kind of food.

It was January 18, 2000, Clinton's last year as president. He showed up at Mike's in Boston's South End neighborhood with Massachusetts senator Ted Kennedy and Mayor Tom Menino, part of a photo opportunity for their work on gun control legislation. The president wore a gray suit with red tie and sat beneath our specials board. Among the choices that day: clam chowder, turkey meatloaf and Boston cream pie.

The two most powerful men in America at the time and the most powerful man in Boston, maybe ever. And they're sitting with me, a 29-year-old immigrant diner cook from Lebanon. They're eating my food, chatting about the Irish peace process. Whitey Bulger. News of the day. Real serious stuff.

Menino served 20 years in office, the longest tenured mayor in Boston history. He was the real deal and people loved him. I loved him.

He was a big supporter of mine because I was one of the first to invest in this part of the South End when I bought Mike's City Diner in 1996. The South End today is one of the trendiest neighborhoods in the country. Beautiful brownstones. High-priced boutiques. Great little chef-driven restaurants. Right next door to Mike's today is Toro, a bustling tapas spot owned by two of my friends, James Beard Award–winning chefs Ken Oringer and Jamie Bissonnette.

But back in 1996 Washington Street was a rough place. Every building around Mike's was boarded up. There were drug dealers on every corner. We'd open at 6 a.m. but I'd keep the metal grates down in front of the windows until 7 just to reduce the likelihood that bullets might fly through the windows. This part of the South End was really that rough at the time. So the mayor showed faith in me because I showed faith in the rejuvenation of Boston. And bringing the president to Mike's City Diner was Menino's very generous way of saying thanks. In fact, the mayor winked at me when I walked in, as if to say, "This one's for you, Jay."

Just a half hour earlier I was at my mom's home in Dedham, southwest of Boston, when Menino's office called to tell me he was bringing the president to Mike's. I ran out of the house and raced into the city. I knew the president was already there by the time I got to the South End because the Secret Service had shut down the streets around the restaurant. So I parked a few blocks away and ran to the security perimeter, where I tried to explain to the agents that I owned the diner.

This was before 9/11 and all the security we have today, but I'm sure my Middle Eastern accent didn't help the situation. I didn't sound like your typical Boston business owner, with that "wicked awesome" local accent.

I called Mike's and one of my employees, Patty, a real tough Southie girl, answered the phone. She grabbed a couple of the agents who were inside the restaurant and they came down to let me in, but only after frisking me first. Some other agents threw me up against my own building and frisked me again before letting me in the door. Then they frisked me a third time before I sat down. Man. I'll tell you. I've been through a lot of scary situations in my life. Shootings. Street fights. Even war itself. Not much makes me nervous. But the power of the president is pretty awe-inspiring. The agents. The limos. Dozens of big black SUVs. There was a guy on the roof guarding the building and a general in the diner standing by the president holding a brief case, I guess in case we had to go to war. I didn't see any guns out in the open. But I assumed the president was surrounded by all kinds of serious firepower. I was shaking by the time I sat down.

Clinton, Kennedy and Menino talked policy while I just sat silently. Soon the conversation turned to the Syria–Israel peace talks. I was a boy in Beirut during the Lebanese Civil War. The Syrians and Israelis backed different factions, of course. My family's little apartment was right in the middle of the combat zone.

One of the neighborhood kids was killed by a Syrian sniper right in front of me. Then there was a massacre of Christians in the Chouf mountains that prompted us to flee to America when I was 8 years old. My grandmother and my uncle were killed in another massacre a few years later.

So Clinton, Kennedy and Menino were talking some heavy-duty stuff about the Middle East crisis. They were talking about the Syrians, the Israelis, the Lebanese. I realized the awesome power we had sitting right there in that room, right there in my diner. I was already nervous to begin with and a little intimidated, too. Now I started to freak out a little.

The president doesn't know I'm Lebanese! I probably shouldn't be listening to this!

Finally, in a fit of nerves, I piped up and told the president that I was from Lebanon. Senator Kennedy was a powerful politician who did so much for so many people around Massachusetts. But he didn't like the way I spoke to the president. He swung out his left arm and he reached out across my chest as if to stop me, then admonished me, like a dad talking to his child: "You don't talk when the president is talking!"

The president didn't say anything to Kennedy, but he could tell I was nervous and now a little embarrassed. But Clinton immediately started talking directly to me like we were old pals. He totally defused the situation. He was brilliant. I was never a Clinton fan before then, not because I didn't like him, but because I wasn't really into politics. But Clinton captured a new fan at that very moment. He just had a way to win you over, like you are the only guy in the room. He was very charismatic.

When he started talking to me, all the nerves went out the window. I didn't even have time to think, "Shit, I'm talking to the president of the United States."

For the next 25 minutes, I shared with President Clinton the story of my life. The war back home. My dad Nicolas running bakeries for the Lebanese army. The bus massacre near our apartment in 1975 that ignited the war. Fleeing into the mountains around Beirut when things got too violent in the city. The escape to America. The tough teenage years brawling on the streets of Boston. Opening my first eatery in nearby Brookline as a teenager and then taking over Mike's City Diner at age 25.

Mike's was doing well at the time the president arrived. People loved our food, my version of cooked-from-scratch American diner classics. It's the food of my adopted homeland and the nation that I love and that gave me and my family incredible opportunities we never would have had back in Lebanon. Mike's City Diner generated more attention as the neighborhood around us gentrified. We got great reviews from the local media.

But that visit from the president really put us on the map. For whatever reason, the story of President Clinton's visit hit the newswires and appeared in papers all over the country, with a picture of the president, the mayor and the senator sitting at one of Mike's four-tops with red checkered tablecloth. It was an all-American scene, a scene that made me very proud then and still makes me very proud today, when I see the diner filled with people from all walks of life, from all over Boston and all over the country.

This book is largely the story I shared with the president that day, told through the food and recipes of my life. It is, at the end of the day, an American success story made possible by hard work, plenty of luck, loving family, caring friends, great food and all the opportunities the United States affords those who come here. It's a country where a poor refugee from a war-torn country overseas might someday sit down and eat with the most powerful man in the world. I'm so proud to be American, because I know this truly is the Land of Opportunity. I'm living proof, as are so many of my friends and so many people from all over the world who come here and succeed every day.

In my case it's a culinary story that begins over a breakfast of ham, grits and eggs with the president of the United States that day back in 2000 at Mike's City Diner.

COOKING NOTES: THE WAY I USE SPICES AND OILS IN ALL MY RECIPES

Spices are best when purchased whole and ground when needed for cooking. In the case of most aromatic spices, such as cardamom, clove and coriander, they are best when first lightly toasted then ground just before cooking. Unless otherwise noted, all recipes in this book call for whole spices to be ground as needed. If you don't have a dedicated spice grinder, an ordinary coffee grinder will work. You can purchase fairly inexpensive grinders online or at any home goods or kitchen store. Your food will taste better, brighter and more flavorful with freshly ground spices.

There is also a big difference between the oils used in this book, especially olive oil and extra virgin olive oil. I use olive oil to cook, stir-fry and sauté food. It actually cooks better than extra virgin olive oil and it's also a lot less expensive.

I use extra virgin olive oil to eat, typically as part of various dips and dressings. The recipes in this book specify when to use regular olive oil or extra virgin olive oil. But generally speaking, use olive oil to cook, use extra virgin olive oil to eat. You'll also see a recipe for ghee, a clarified butter used in Middle Eastern cooking that I often use as a substitute for other oils when cooking or sautéing food.

CREAMY COUNTRY GRITS

These are the same creamy country-style grits that President Clinton ate here at Mike's City Diner. Few eateries here in New England serve grits. In fact, Mike's is one of the few places in Boston to find them. But I like grits because they're simple and hearty and because you can flavor them a thousand different ways. My favorite way is to break in a couple runny poached eggs with salt and pepper. For a little New England flavor, mix some country sausage in with your grits and douse with real maple syrup.

4 cups (946 ml) water
2 tbsp (28 g) unsalted butter, divided
1 tsp salt
1 cup (156 g) stoneground grits
½ cup (120 ml) heavy cream

Pour the water into a heavy, 4-quart (4-L) saucepan with 1 tablespoon (14 g) of butter and the salt and bring to a boil. Stir in the grits and reduce the heat to low. Cover and stir frequently, adding more water as needed if the grits get too thick and too dry, about 40 minutes. Remove from the heat and stir in the cream and remaining tablespoon (14 g) of butter. Serve as a side with your favorite eggs or breakfast meats.

HOUSE-CURED CORNED BEEF

MAKES UP TO 5 LBS (2.2 KG)

The Irish were mostly poor when they flooded Boston in the nineteenth century, much like my family was poor when we arrived in the 1970s. They were reduced to buying and eating cheap, tough cuts of beef, like brisket. They "corned" the beef—basically, a simple curing process—to make the brisket more tender and tasty. Corned beef remains hugely popular in Boston today. In fact, there is even a New England–style gray corned beef you find only in this part of the country. It's very easy to cure your own corned beef at home. And the results are delicious!

PICKLING SPICES

1 tbsp (9 g) whole peppercorns

1 tbsp (10 g) whole mustard seed

½ tbsp (3 g) whole coriander

½ tsp whole juniper

½ tsp whole allspice

½ tsp whole clove

½ stick of cinnamon

3 bay leaves

BRINE

8 cups (2 L) cold water

1 cup (135 g) kosher salt

¼ cup (55 g) brown sugar

½ tsp garlic powder

3 garlic cloves

Optional: 1 tsp Insta Cure No. 1 or pink salt (use for red corned beef; omit for New England-style gray corned beef)

BRISKET

2½ to 5 lb (1 to 2 kg) fresh brisket

2 tsp (10 ml) vegetable oil

1 onion, quartered

2 cloves garlic

To make the pickling spices, mix the spices together in a bowl. Take half of the spices and lightly crush them with a mortar and pestle. Or, put half the spices in a heavy-duty resealable bag and lightly crush them with rolling pin against a hard surface. Crush all of the spices if you so choose, but at least half. Bay leaves can be broken up by hand.

Pour cold water into a ceramic crock or other nonreactive, food-grade container. Set aside 2 teaspoons (10 g) of the pickling spices for later. Stir in the remaining pickling spices, salt, brown sugar, garlic powder, garlic cloves and optional Insta Cure No. 1 until all is dissolved. Now add the meat so that it's submerged.

Put something heavy on top of the meat to keep it submerged (a plate will do the trick). Cover the crock and place in the refrigerator or a cool dry place (the basement should be fine) for 8 to 10 days.

Remove the meat from the brine and rinse. Preheat the oven to 275°F (135°C). Pour the vegetable oil in a large Dutch oven over high heat. When the oil starts to shimmer, sear each side of brisket, about 6 to 7 minutes per side, until well browned. Transfer the meat to a large roasting pan and add enough water to cover the brisket by 1 inch (2.5 cm). Add in the reserved 2 teaspoons (10 g) of reserved pickling spices. Wrap the pan tightly with aluminum foil. Bake in oven for 3½ to 4 hours, until the meat is very tender. Let cool for about 10 minutes then slice the meat against the grain and serve with your favorite potatoes and vegetables.

SOUTHERN-STYLE SHRIMP & GRITS

SERVES 4

Mike's City Diner is a Boston institution, but there's a vein of southern flavor that courses through the menu. Every now and then we gussy up our grits with some southern-style shrimp. For a little added kick, coat the shrimp in Old Bay before and/or after cooking them.

5 slices thick, high-quality bacon, cut into ¼- to ½-inch (6- to 12-mm) pieces

2 tbsp (14 g) finely chopped red bell pepper

1 lb (454 g) medium shrimp, peeled and deveined

3 cloves garlic, crushed

1 tsp freshly chopped parsley

5 scallions, thinly sliced

1 tbsp (15 ml) fresh lemon juice

Creamy Country Grits (see page 18)

Fry the bacon in a large skillet over medium-high heat until browned, about 4 to 6 minutes. Remove the bacon with a slotted spoon and set aside, leaving the grease in the pan. Sauté the bell pepper in the fat for about 1 minute, stirring regularly. Add the shrimp and garlic and sauté 2 to 3 minutes, stirring regularly until the shrimp takes on an even pinkish hue. Add the parsley, scallions and lemon juice and return the bacon to the pan. Sauté for an additional 2 to 3 minutes, stirring to mix together all the ingredients well. Spoon the grits into four bowls. Pile the shrimp mixture in the center of each bowl.

BISCUITS & CHORIZO GRAVY

Biscuits & gravy is a classic American breakfast dish, but one that's not very common in Northeastern cities like Boston. In fact, Mike's City Diner is one of the few places in the city where you can get good old-fashioned, down-home biscuits & sausage gravy—a creamy pork-filled sauce poured all over fresh, fluffy biscuits.

We like to spice it up a little, though, and make the sausage gravy with a chorizo spice blend. Greater Boston has huge Spanish- and Portuguese-speaking communities. So this gravy is kind of a cross-cultural version of a great American breakfast classic.

BISCUITS

2 cups (240 g) all-purpose flour

1 tbsp (15 g) baking powder

1 tsp sugar

1 tsp salt

6 tbsp (90 g) very cold unsalted butter, cut into small cubes

1 cup (235 ml) whole milk

2 egg whites

CHORIZO GRAVY

¼ cup (60 ml) apple cider vinegar

4 cloves garlic, crushed

2 tsp (4 g) chili powder

2 tsp (4 g) salt

½ tsp oregano

1 tsp cumin

½ tsp coriander

1½ tsp (7 g) black pepper

1 tsp paprika

1 lb (450 g) ground pork

1 tbsp (15 ml) olive oil

⅓ cup (40 g) flour

4 cups (945 ml) milk

Preheat oven to 425°F (218°C). Whisk together the flour, baking powder, sugar and salt. Cut in butter with your fingers until the flour takes on a granular texture. Add the milk and mix into the dough as little as is needed to bind the dough together. Do not overmix. Roll out the dough on a floured surface, about ½- to ¾-inch (6.5- to 13-cm) thick. Cut biscuits with 3-inch (7.5-cm) round cookie or biscuit cutter. You should get 8 to 9 biscuits. You can also roll out the dough into a square and cut in a tic-tac-toe pattern to create 9 square biscuits. Scramble the egg whites, then brush on top of each biscuit. Bake 10 to 14 minutes, depending on thickness.

Whisk the vinegar together with garlic and spices. Mix pork together well with the vinegar and spices in a medium bowl, ensuring spices are evenly distributed through the meat. Refrigerate at least 3 hours or overnight.

Pour olive oil in medium-sized heavy sauce pan over medium-high heat. Add meat and brown well, stirring occasionally while breaking up the meat, about 6 to 8 minutes. Reduce heat. Add flour to meat and cook an additional 2 minutes, stirring constantly, until flour is lightly browned. Whisk in milk until smooth and simmer about 10 minutes until thickened. If too thick, add a little water or black coffee to achieve desired texture. Pour over fresh biscuits.

MAYOR MENINO'S ROASTED VEGETABLE ITALIAN OMELET

The late Tom Menino was the longest-serving mayor in the history of Boston and one of my biggest supporters. He ate at Mike's City Diner all the time and brought President Clinton here as a way to say thanks for my investment in the South End community. I owe a lot to Mayor Menino, as do all the citizens of Boston, for the incredible work he did to revitalize the city over the past couple of decades. Menino was and remains the only Italian-American to serve as the mayor of Boston. So I made this omelet in tribute to his heritage.

VEGETABLES

1 small eggplant, ½-inch (12-mm) dice

1 medium zucchini, ½-inch (12-mm) dice

1 medium summer squash, ½-inch (12-mm) dice

1 small red onion, medium dice

1 red pepper, medium dice

8 oz (224 g) cherry tomatoes, halved

2 tbsp (30 ml) extra virgin olive oil

1 tsp dried thyme

½ tsp salt

½ tsp freshly ground black pepper

OMELET

3 eggs

Dash of olive oil

2 slices provolone cheese

To roast the vegetables, preheat the oven to 400°F (204°C). Line a large baking sheet with parchment paper. Place the eggplant, zucchini, squash, onion, pepper and tomatoes in a large bowl. Drizzle with olive oil and sprinkle with thyme, salt and pepper. Toss to coat the vegetables. Pour the mixture onto the baking sheet in a single layer. Bake 25 to 30 minutes, or to desired tenderness. Hot vegetables can be used immediately to make omelets, or set them aside and refrigerate until ready to cook. These vegetables will make about 8 to 10 omelets. However, these roasted veggies can also be used as a delicious and healthy side to grilled meats.

To make the omelet, whisk the eggs in a bowl. Splash the olive oil onto a good nonstick sauté pan over medium heat. Pour the eggs into a sauté pan and heat them gently until almost cooked through. The time it takes to cook through will vary depending on the size of the pan and the heat. But you'll see the eggs firm up, of course, as they cook through. Along the way, gently lift the edges of the omelet and lift the pan so that still liquefied egg on the top moves to the bottom of the pan. This will help the omelet cook through faster.

When the eggs are firm and about cooked through, if you're confident enough, flip the eggs by quickly snapping the pan upward with a flick of the wrist. Otherwise, use a spatula to gently flip the eggs. Or, you can simply let the eggs cook through. Place ½ cup (120 g) of the hot vegetables on half the eggs. (If the vegetables were refrigerated, simply reheat them first in a separate sauté pan.) Place the provolone on top of the vegetables. Pour the omelet onto a plate, flipping, with the pan or with a spatula, the uncovered half of the eggs over the top of the vegetables and cheese to close up the omelet.

MIKE'S CLASSIC BACON FAT HOME FRIES

Guests at Mike's City Diner wolf down hundreds of pounds of home fries each and every week. And they often wonder what the secret is. Well, it's very simple. We cook our home fries in bacon fat! Maybe not the healthiest secret, but certainly delicious.

SEASONING SALT

1 tbsp (17 g) kosher salt

1 tbsp (7 g) white pepper

1 tbsp (7 g) onion powder

1 tbsp (7 g) garlic powder

1 tbsp (7 g) Spanish paprika

HOME FRIES

4 Yukon gold potatoes, with skin

1 medium yellow onion, diced

2 tbsp (30 ml) bacon fat, divided

2 tbsp (30 ml) olive oil, divided

1 tbsp (10 g) seasoning salt

To make the seasoning salt, mix together all the ingredients and store in an airtight container until ready to use.

To make the home fries, boil the potatoes whole until cooked through, about 15 minutes. Let them cool. Then chop the potatoes into ½-inch (12-mm) chunks. Sauté the onion in half the bacon fat and half the olive oil over medium-high heat until translucent, about 5 minutes. Add the potatoes, seasoning salt and the remaining bacon fat and olive oil. Heat until lightly browned on one side, about 5 minutes. Then flip the potatoes and continue to cook on the other side until browned and crispy, about 10 minutes.

HOME-CURED BONE-IN HAM

SERVES 6 TO 10

People talk a lot about our turkeys. But it was actually our hand-carved, bone-in ham that first put Mike's City Diner on the map. Soon after I bought the restaurant we got a call from the great folks at *Chronicle*, a popular Boston-area TV show on WCVB Channel 5 that reports on food, travel and lifestyle topics around New England. *Chronicle* has been on the air forever and people love the show. They had apparently heard about hand-carved ham, which at the time was something of a novelty—kind of like our fresh-cooked turkeys. That first bit of exposure at a time when the South End was still struggling to redevelop really helped the the diner and helped the neighborhood. We still serve the same hand-carved ham on the bone today. You'll find it in the Mike's Special breakfast, in our other breakfast and lunch sandwiches and as a side to any dish you want. You can even make it yourself at home.

3 cups (405 g) kosher salt

3 cups (330 g) brown sugar

1 tbsp (12 g) each black peppercorns, whole coriander, whole cumin, fennel seed and red pepper flakes (or ½ cup [60 g] pickling spice, page 19)

4 to 5 bay leaves

2 tbsp plus 2 tsp (45 g) Insta Cure No. 1 or Pink Salt No. 1

2 quarts (1.8 L) water

1½ gallons (9.4 L) icy water

10 to 14 lb (4.5 to 6.3 kg) fresh, bone-in ham

OPTIONAL GLAZE

1 cup (230 g) Dijon mustard

1 cup (230 g) honey

1 pinch salt

1 pinch cayenne pepper

Place the salt, brown sugar, spices, bay leaves and Insta Cure or pink salt in large ceramic crock or food-grade plastic bucket, big enough to hold all the liquid and the ham with at least several inches to spare at the top of the container. Bring the water to a boil and pour over the ingredients in the container. Whisk to dissolve the salt and sugar. Pour in the icy water to quickly cool the mixture.

Score the skin of the ham with a sharp knife in several places, 1 inch (2.5 cm) apart, cutting into the fat but not into the meat below. Make a perpendicular cut against each score to create a diamond pattern.

If possible, inject the ham all over with the cool brine with a high-quality, food-grade injection needle. You should see the ham expand as you inject the brine. Lower the ham into the brine, skin side up. Refrigerate 1 day for every 2 pounds (900 g) of pork; half the time if you have injected the brine into the ham. After the ham is cured, discard the brine, rinse the salt off the ham and soak in the same container in fresh cold water at least a couple hours or overnight.

Preheat the oven to 325°F (163°C). Add 1 cup (235 ml) of water to a large roasting pan. Remove the roast from the water and pat dry with towels. Roast the ham on a rack until it reaches an internal temperature of 135°F (57°C), about 4 hours depending upon size.

Mix the mustard, honey, salt and pepper together in a medium-sized bowl and set aside.

Add another cup (235 ml) of water to the pan if it has dried up. Increase oven to 425°F (218°C) and continue to roast until the skin is browned and crispy and internal temperature reaches 150°F (65°C), about 30 to 45 minutes. Brush ham generously with glaze, if using, and return to oven for 5 to 10 minutes.

Remove the ham, tent with aluminum foil and let it rest for 25 to 30 minutes before slicing.

CORNED BEEF HASH WITH CRATER-POACHED EGGS

Corned beef tastes great on its own, but it's even better when it's chopped up and mixed with potatoes and spices to create corned beef hash, which is ubiquitous in breakfast joints around Boston. It was only later in life that I realized that different parts of the country have different kinds of hash—if they have it at all—and that corned beef hash is a regional breakfast specialty here in New England. We make all kinds of hash here at Mike's, including turkey hash and duck hash. But corned beef hash is one of the foundations of our breakfast menu. This recipe is a great way to use all that corned beef you have left over after St. Patrick's Day.

1 lb (454 g) boiled Yukon gold or favorite potatoes

1 lb (454 g) favorite cooked corned beef

4 tbsp (56 g) unsalted butter

1 yellow onion, diced medium

1 tbsp (4 g) finely chopped parsley

¼ tsp cinnamon

½ tsp nutmeg

1 tsp salt

Black pepper to taste

1 clove garlic, minced

¼ cup (60 ml) beef stock (or chicken stock)

4 eggs

Boil just enough water to cover the potatoes in a medium stock pot. Add the potatoes and simmer until fork tender, about 15 to 20 minutes. Remove and mash half the potatoes and roughly chop the other half. Set aside.

Roughly chop half the corned beef. Finely chop the remaining half, or grind it fine in a food processor for a finer textured hash.

Heat the butter to medium-high in a 12-inch (30.5-cm) cast-iron skillet. Sauté the onions and roughly chopped potatoes until browned, about 5 to 6 minutes. Stir in the corned beef, parsley, cinnamon, nutmeg, salt and pepper. Stir occasionally until all of the mixture is browned. Add the garlic and mashed potatoes. Mix well. Add the stock and let cook 1 minute, while stirring to ensure all of it is equally mixed. Using a spatula, press down on the corned beef mixture until flat and even. Sauté about 10 minutes until crispy underneath. Flip the entire mixture, in sections if needed. Flatten again until even.

Now, using the back of a large spoon, press down to create four rounded craters in the corned beef mixture. Crack an egg into each crater. Cover the pan tightly and cook until the eggs are set, about 5 minutes.

BEEF SHORT RIB SHEPHERD'S PIE

SERVES 6

This is not your average shepherd's pie. It's a richer, more savory version I usually make for special occasions only at home, occasions that call for some true comfort food. Maybe a chilly winter day with the family or entertaining friends during the Patriots game. This shepherd's pie also has one of my signature touches—a splash of pomegranate syrup.

4 lb (1816 g) bone-in beef short ribs

Salt and pepper to taste

3 tbsp (45 ml) olive oil

4 cups (640 g) diced yellow onion

1½ cups (200 g) roughly chopped carrots

½ cup (50 g) chopped celery

5 cloves garlic, chopped

2 tbsp (30 ml) tomato paste

3 tbsp (15 g) all-purpose flour

2 cups (473 ml) dry red wine

2 tbsp (30 ml) pomegranate syrup

2½ cups (600 ml) beef stock

2 bay leaves

1 tsp dry thyme

1 tsp oregano

1 tsp rosemary

2 cups (170 g) portobello mushrooms, diced large

1½ cups (200 g) chopped parsnip

3 lb (1362) russet potatoes, peeled and quartered

1 cup (240 ml) milk

1 stick (112 g) butter

2 tsp (12 g) salt, or to taste

½ tsp pepper, or to taste

3 tbsp (10 g) chopped fresh parsley

1 egg, beaten

To make the short ribs, begin by peeling the thin, fibrous membrane off the back of the ribs. A paper towel will help, as the membrane is hard to grip with bare hands. Then season the ribs well with salt and pepper. Heat the oil over medium-high heat until almost shimmering and then sear ribs until browned on all sides. Cook in batches if needed so not to overcrowd the pan. Set the ribs aside. Add the onion, carrots, celery and garlic and sauté until translucent, about 10 minutes, stirring constantly. Add the tomato paste and stir until the vegetables are well mixed with the paste. Stir in the flour until combined and the mixture becomes a thick roux, constantly mixing, about 3 minutes. The flour should brown but not burn. Add the wine and heat until it boils, stirring well to deglaze the pan, scraping up brown bits. Add the syrup and beef stock and stir. Mix in the bay leaves, thyme, oregano and rosemary. Return the short ribs to the pan with any juices from the meat. Bring the mixture to a boil. Add the mushrooms and parsnips. Cover and reduce to simmer for 90 minutes.

Prepare the mashed potatoes while the meat is simmering for 90 minutes. Boil the potatoes in enough salted water to cover the potatoes by 2 to 3 inches (5 to 7.5 cm), for 15 to 20 minutes. Drain well. Turn the potatoes through a ricer or mash by hand. Scald milk and butter in a small sauce pan until almost boiling. Stir the scalded milk and butter into the potatoes. Add salt and pepper. Set aside.

Remove the meat from the mixture with a slotted spoon after it has for simmered 90 minutes. Debone the short ribs—the meat should fall from the bone easily—and remove any remaining fibers. Dice the meat into ¾-inch (1.9-cm) cubes. Return the meat to the pot with parsley. Cook another 30 minutes, uncovered, until liquid is reduced and very thick, but not dry.

Preheat the oven to 400°F (204°C) while the short rib mixture is simmering for the final 30 minutes. Pour the finished short rib mixture into a large 3-inch (8-cm) tall casserole dish and spread evenly with a spatula. Spread the mashed potatoes across top of mixture. Brush the egg over the top of the potatoes. Bake for about 30 minutes. If you want even more flavor, refrigerate the pie overnight in the casserole dish and then bake the following day. Garnish with parsley.

BULGUR-CRUSTED FRIED CHICKEN WITH ALEPPO PEPPER

SERVES 4 TO 6

There is nothing more American than good, old-fashioned fried chicken. I add a little global flavor to the fried chicken at Mike's, by crusting it in bulgur and adding a splash of mildly hot Aleppo pepper, a staple of Middle Eastern cooking that I love and that's growing in popularity here in the United States. I use thighs simply because they're move flavorful than the breasts. I love making this dish at various functions, fundraisers and tastings, typically serving the chicken on slider buns with slaw, pickles and spicy mayo. It's a true crowd pleaser!

Cooking oil

½ cup (70 g) No. 1–grade fine bulgur

2 cups (250 g) all-purpose flour

1 tbsp (7 g) onion powder

1 tbsp (7 g) garlic powder

1 tbsp (7 g) Aleppo pepper

2 tbsp (34 g) kosher salt, divided

3 eggs

1 tbsp (7 g) black pepper

2 lb (908 g) boneless chicken thighs

Heat 2 to 3 inches (5 to 7.5 cm) of oil to 350°F (176°C) in a deep, heavy pot.

Blend the bulgur in a food processor on high for 1 minute to break it down even more finely. Add the flour, onion powder, garlic powder, Aleppo pepper and 1 tablespoon (17 g) kosher salt and blend again until all is mixed together, about 10 seconds. Pour the mixture into a shallow dish or pan.

Beat the eggs with the remaining salt and pepper and place in a separate pan. Dip the chicken thighs in the egg mixture, making sure all parts of the chicken are well coated. Dredge the chicken in the flour mixture until all sides and crevices are coated. Gently place the chicken in hot oil and fry for about 7 to 9 minutes.

For extra crispy chicken, remove the chicken from the oil after 6 minutes. Let the chicken cool to room temperature, then refrigerate at least a couple of hours or overnight. When ready to serve, re-fry chicken in oil for 3 to 3½ minutes. Do not overcook, or the chicken will dry out and the breading will turn too dark.

CONFIT DUCK HASH

SERVES TO 2 TO 4

We added confit duck hash to the menu at Mike's City Diner in 2016 and it was an instant hit. It is the Cadillac of hashes: rich, luxurious and, yes, a little more expensive than other kinds of hash. Still, our guests absolutely love it. We get our duck confit specially prepared for us by Bella Bella Gourmet Foods of Connecticut, which represents duck farmers in upstate New York. But these days you can find confit duck at most specialty markets and even many local supermarkets.

2½ lb (1135 g) potatoes
2 tbsp (30 ml) olive oil
1 red pepper, diced small
1 large yellow onion, diced small
2 cloves garlic, finely chopped
1 cup (128 g) shredded carrots
1 rib of celery, diced small
2 cups (480 ml) chicken stock
1½ tsp (1 g) fresh thyme
1 lb (454 g) shredded duck confit
¼ cup (15 g) chopped parsley

Boil just enough water to cover the potatoes in a medium stock pot. Add the potatoes and simmer until fork tender, about 15 to 20 minutes. Remove and mash half the potatoes and roughly chop the other half. Set aside.

Heat the oil until shimmering in a medium-sized sauce pan. Add the pepper and sauté over high heat until the edges start to turn black. Add the onion and garlic. Sauté 3 to 4 minutes until onion turns lightly brown. Stir in the carrots and celery and sauté 1 more minute. Add stock and thyme and stir to deglaze the pan. Add the pre-boiled potatoes immediately and stir to soften.

Once the liquid starts to thicken, add the confit and mix well until it forms into a thick hash. Once the duck is warmed through, turn off the heat and add the parsley. Mix well. Refrigerate overnight to let the flavors develop.

When ready to cook, ladle the hash into a hot pan with a little ghee, butter or oil and press flat. Cook about 5 to 8 minutes until the hash is crispy. Flip, flatten and repeat. Top with poached or runny fried eggs, if you'd like.

BUCKWHEAT PANCAKES WITH COCONUT WHIPPED CREAM

We sell a LOT of pancakes at Mike's City Diner, typically serving them with fresh fruit. I created this pancake made with buckwheat to give our guests a gluten-free version. Some Mike's City Diner fans say it's the perfect pancake: wisps of house-made coconut whipped cream, plenty of sweet syrup and the nutritious energy of buckwheat, which is actually a seed and not real wheat, which makes these fluffy pancakes both gluten free and delicious.

COCONUT CREAM

2 (14-oz [414-ml]) cans unsweetened coconut milk

2 tsp (10 ml) vanilla extract

2 tbsp (16 g) powdered sugar

PANCAKES

2 cups (240 g) buckwheat flour

1½ tbsp (17 g) sugar

2 tsp (9 g) baking powder

½ tsp salt

1 large egg

1½ tbsp (21 g) melted butter

½ tsp vanilla extract

2½ cups (600 ml) buttermilk or whole milk

To make the coconut cream, pour both cans of coconut milk into a see-through plastic container. Refrigerate overnight to separate cream from water. Place in the freezer for 1 hour right before preparing whipped cream. Scoop out the cream solids, leaving the ice water behind, and place the cream in a cold mixing bowl. Refrigerate the water to drink or use later. Whip the cream with an electric beater until peaks start to form, about 5 to 10 minutes. As soon as the peaks form, add the vanilla and sugar. Beat for another 30 seconds to 1 minute.

Place the flour, sugar, baking powder and salt in a bowl and whisk together. In a separate bowl, whisk together the egg, butter, vanilla and buttermilk until well incorporated. Pour the wet mixture into the dry mixture. Stir together very well. Pour 2 ounces (60 g) of batter per pancake onto a hot seasoned griddle. The pancake is ready to flip when bubbles pop up on top side. Flip and cook about 1 more minute. Top each pancake with 1 tablespoon (15 g) of coconut cream.

See image on page 12.

CLASSIC BOSTON CREAM PIE

SERVES 8

Boston cream pie was one of our blackboard specials the day that President Clinton arrived for breakfast with Senator Kennedy and Mayor Menino. This iconic Boston recipe, a double layer sponge cake filled with pastry cream and topped with chocolate icing, was developed just down the road from Mike's City Diner at what's now the Omni Parker House Hotel. It's the same place that invented the Parker House dinner roll. Boston cream pie is such a classic that I don't mess with it. I've simply followed the original Parker House recipe, which I first discovered many years ago and still use today.

CAKE

7 eggs

8 oz (224 g) sugar, divided

1 cup (125 g) flour

1 oz (28 g) melted butter

PASTRY CREAM

1 tbsp (14 g) butter

2 cups (480 ml) milk

2 cups (480 ml) light cream

½ cup (100 g) sugar

3½ tbsp (28 g) cornstarch

6 eggs

1 tsp dark rum

ICING

5 oz (140 g) white fondant

6 oz (168 g) chocolate fondant

3 oz (84 g) semi-sweet chocolate, melted

Preheat the oven to 350°F (176°C).

To make the cake, separate the egg yolks and whites into two separate bowls. Add half of the sugar to each bowl. Beat both until peaked. When stiff, fold the whites into the yolk mixture. Gradually add the flour, mixing with a wooden spatula. Mix in the butter. Pour this mixture into a 10-inch (25-cm) round greased cake pan. Bake for about 20 minutes, or until spongy and golden. Remove from the oven and allow to cool fully.

To make the pastry cream, boil the butter, milk and light cream in a sauce pan. While this mixture is cooking, combine the sugar, cornstarch and eggs in a bowl and whip until ribbons form. When the cream, milk and butter mixture reaches the boiling point, whisk in the egg mixture and cook to boiling again. Boil for 1 minute. Pour into a bowl and cover the surface with plastic wrap. Refrigerate overnight if possible. When chilled, whisk to smooth out and flavor with the dark rum.

For the icing, warm the white fondant in a double broiler over boiling water to about 105°F (40°C). Thin with water if necessary so that the icing can be piped easily. Place in a piping bag with an ⅛-inch (3-mm) tip. Then warm the chocolate fondant over boiling water to about 105°F (40°C), then stir in the melted chocolate. Set aside.

Cut the cake into two layers. Spread the flavored pastry cream over the bottom layer. Top with the second cake layer. Spread a thin layer of chocolate fondant icing on the top of the cake. Then use the white fondant in the pastry bag to create spiral lines starting from the center of the cake. Then score the lines with a paring knife, pulling outward toward the edge of the cake to create almost a spider web effect. There you have it—Boston cream pie!

CHAPTER 2

Pâté During Wartime in Beirut

My old neighborhood in Beirut enjoys a poetic name: Ain el-Remmaneh in Arabic, "The Eye of the Pomegranate" in English. It sounds pleasant.

The Eye of the Pomegranate was anything but pleasant, however. The Eye of the Storm might describe it better. It was here in this neighborhood, not far from my family's small fourth-floor apartment, that Beirut's bloody Bus Massacre of 1975 killed dozens of people and ignited the Lebanese Civil War.

I was just 5 years old then, and we were in the heart of the fighting, one faction camped outside the back of our building and another in the front. Bullets flew and bombs exploded and we were in the crosshairs. We'd run for shelter, either to a lower floor, to the elevator shaft or to a neighbor's house and eventually, when things got really bad, up into the Lebanon mountains.

The violence never scared me. Not because I was brave or tough, but because as a boy, it's all I knew. The war was just a fact of life and we all lived with it. As kids we actually looked forward to the fighting, because it meant a day off from school. Then after the fighting we'd sweep the streets looking for souvenirs: brass bullet casings, discarded combat equipment, shrapnel fragments, things like that. We'd pile everything in buckets to see who scored the biggest stash.

It was an adventure to us. It was only later, in the comfort of America, raising my own four children, that I realized how scary it was and how painful it must have been for my dad Nicolas and my mom Samira to raise a family amid the bloodshed. It never dawned on me as a child that they must have been worried sick. Certainly, it was their concern for their four children, my sister Micheline, brothers Elias and Michael, and me, the baby of the family, that inspired them to flee for the strange land of the United States.

Food was always a challenge, of course. Food is scarce to begin with in a war-torn city like Beirut. On top of its scarcity, we never knew when we'd have to flee and we never knew how long we'd be gone. It might be hours. It might be days.

My dad was in the Army and often away fighting the war. When something bad happened, he'd race out of the house with all his weapons. Mom had to feed four children no matter the circumstances. Her shelter food of choice were tin cans of pâté that opened up with a key, the way you used to get sardines here in America. She could throw a few cans in a bag with some pita bread or baguettes and have enough to feed us for days if needed.

People here in America think of pâté as a luxury item you eat at gastropubs and fine restaurants. But when I was boy pâtés and terrines were a bare necessity: something poor families ate just to survive the war.

We could eat this mixture of ground liver, meat and spices right out of the can, like you might see in old films of American GIs from World War II eating tin-can C-rations. Mom would often spread the pâté on *saj* or pita bread so we could eat it like a sandwich and maybe pair it with some simple homemade *labneh* cheese, which she stored in jars of olive oil and often stuffed in the same survival bag. Or, if we were really lucky, we'd spread the cheese or pâté between a beautiful French baguette. Lebanon was a French colony for many years and it created a rather unique blend of Arabic and European influences that still impacts my cooking today.

Those pâté sandwiches are my earliest food memory and something I still make for friends today—only from scratch instead of out of a can and not in a dark shelter, but in the comfort and safety of our warm American home.

POMEGRANATE, ONION & BACON MARMALADE

Pâté tastes best when you serve it with something sweet to cut through all that delicious, rich, savory fat. I created this delicious pomegranate-flavored marmalade to pair perfectly with my Chicken Liver Pâté (page 42) and to pay tribute to my childhood neighborhood in Beirut, Ain el-Remmaneh (the Eye of the Pomegranate).

6 slices hardwood-smoked, thick-cut bacon

2 tbsp (30 ml) olive oil

3 large sweet yellow onions, sliced ¼-inch (6-mm) thick

1 cup (200 g) sugar

2 tbsp (30 ml) balsamic vinegar

½ cup (120 ml) pomegranate juice

Dash of kosher salt

Preheat the oven to 400°F (204°C). Place the bacon flat on a sheet pan. Bake about 20 minutes until bacon is very crispy. Remove the bacon from the grease and set it aside to cool on paper towels.

Heat the oil in a medium sauce pan over medium-high heat until the oil is shimmering. Add the onions and sauté, stirring occasionally, until golden brown, about 15 minutes. Slowly sprinkle the sugar over the onions and let cook, without stirring, until the sugar melts, about 5 minutes. Increase the heat to high and cook, without stirring, until amber brown caramel forms, about 6 minutes. Stir in the vinegar and pomegranate juice, reduce the heat to low and simmer, stirring a few minutes, until marmalade is thick, about 5 more minutes. Add the salt, crumble the bacon and sprinkle into the mixture. Stir gently to incorporate. Let cool to room temperature, then refrigerate until ready to use.

CHICKEN LIVER PÂTÉ

MAKES ABOUT 2 CUPS (170 G)

Pâté will always remind me of those days hiding out in the shelters of Beirut, wondering when we might head back home. I've since grown to love making pâté at home here in Boston, though my version is more like a chicken liver mousse. Regardless, it's delicious. It keeps a long time when stored properly. And, well, people think it's fancy food when, in reality, it's the stuff we ate to survive back during the war.

1 medium onion, finely chopped

2 cloves garlic

14 tbsp (196 g) very cold unsalted butter, cut into ½-inch (12-mm) cubes, then warmed to room temperature, divided

1 tbsp (15 ml) vegetable oil

1 lb (454 g) fresh chicken livers, trimmed

¼ cup (60 ml) bourbon

1 tbsp (2 g) chopped fresh thyme

1 tsp (2 g) freshly ground allspice

Kosher salt to taste

6 tbsp (90 ml) heavy cream, plus more if needed

Optional: rendered duck fat as needed

Sauté the onion with the garlic in 1 tablespoon (14 g) of butter over medium heat until translucent, about 5 or 6 minutes, being careful not to burn the garlic. Transfer to a plate.

Pour the vegetable oil in the sauté pan and bring to almost smoking hot. Sauté the livers by gently shaking them around in hot oil until lightly browned on all sides, about 5 minutes. Lower the heat and pour in the bourbon. But be careful, the pan should flare up quickly from the alcohol. Remove the pan from the heat source after 1 minute.

Place the livers and any remaining liquid in a food processor with the onion and garlic mixture. Add thyme, allspice and salt. Start blending and add the remaining butter, cube by cube, until all has been added. Then start pouring in the cream slowly and puree until all ingredients are very well incorporated. Pour the warm liquid into a mason jar and chill for at least two hours. Optional: for cleaner tasting pâté, sift the warm liquid through a fine-mesh strainer to remove any hard solids, then pour into a mason jar and chill.

Keep the pâté refrigerated until ready to use. To keep pâté fresh for an extended period, fill the extra space in the mason jar with duck fat and chill. The fat will protect the pâté from oxygen and, therefore, keep it from going stale. Serve this pâté as part of a charcuterie plate, or spread on a baguette or pita bread with Homestyle Labneh (see page 53) or my signature Pomegranate, Onion & Bacon Marmalade (page 41).

KOFTA KEBABS

SERVES 6 TO 8

Back home these family-style kebabs were typically made with lamb. Lebanon is so small and mountainous that it's not really conducive to large-scale cattle farming. But here in the United States, I almost always make these kebabs with ground beef only, mainly because beef is so plentiful and because my kids prefer it to lamb. However, feel free to make this dish with lamb, a 50/50 mix of ground beef and ground lamb or just with beef. In either case, make sure the meat is at least 20 percent fat for a richer, more savory flavor. It will cook better on the grill, too.

3 lb (1362 g) 80/20 finely ground beef

1 medium yellow onion, blended or very finely chopped

1 bunch of parsley leaves, ⅔ of stems removed, finely chopped

1 tbsp (6 g) allspice

2 tsp (4 g) nutmeg

2 tsp (4 g) cinnamon

1 tsp ground ginger

2 tsp (4 g) fine black pepper

2 tbsp (36 g) kosher salt

4 cloves garlic

Mix all the ingredients together very well in a large bowl. Refrigerate for 4 hours or overnight. Grab chunks of the mixture, about 3 ounces (84 g) each, and roll into a ball. Place each meatball on a metal or soaked bamboo skewer (you'll need about 15 skewers and the bamboo should be soaked at least 1 hour). Lengthen the meat into an elongated kebab shape on the skewers with lightly wet hands. Have a bowl of cold water handy to keep your hands wet. Grill over a medium-hot charcoal or gas fire, searing the meat on all sides, about 2 to 3 minutes per side.

Slide the meat off the skewer onto a platter. Serve with Hashweh (see page 49), Freekeh Fattoush Salad (page 98) or tabouli salad.

Note: It's important that the beef or lamb in this recipe is finely ground, more finely ground than typical hamburger meat. It's easier to form over the skewers and makes for a smoother texture that grills more easily and tastes better, too. Ask your butcher for fine-ground meat before making this recipe.

MARINATED CHICKEN KEBABS

SERVES 4 TO 6

Roof-top grilling is a big part of the food and family culture in Lebanon. Basically, people turn their roofs into a patio and cook and eat outside. Some of my earliest childhood memories are hanging out with my mom's family in the mountains of Chouf, or my dad's family in Machghara, eating on the roof. We always had a little hibachi and it seems there were always some kebabs sizzling away. Typically, kebabs were served "family style"—that is, we filled a big plate with a variety of kebabs, such as Kofta Kebabs (see page 45), Muhamarah Duck Kebabs (see page 52) and these lemony marinated chicken kebabs.

¼ cup (60 ml) fresh lemon juice

¼ cup (60 ml) olive oil

1 tbsp (18 g) kosher salt

2 tsp (4 g) Aleppo pepper

1 tsp paprika

1 tsp allspice

½ tsp cumin

½ tsp cinnamon

¼ tsp cayenne

4 cloves garlic, crushed

2 lb (908) boneless, skinless chicken thighs, cut into 2-inch (5-cm) cubes

Mix together the lemon juice, oil, salt, spices and garlic in a large resealable bag. Add the cubed chicken. Make sure all the air is pushed out of the bag. Marinate in the refrigerator for at least 4 hours but preferably overnight. Soak bamboo skewers for at least an hour to prevent them from burning on the grill, or use steel skewers. Carefully weave each piece of chicken onto a skewer in two different places so that the meat will not spin when rotating the skewers. Heat the grill to medium high. Grill the chicken on two to three sides, about 3 to 4 minutes per side, until grill marks form and chicken is cooked through. Serve with grilled vegetables, tahini or salad, or roll between pita bread with lettuce, tomatoes, pickles and tahini.

HASHWEH (LEBANESE RICE)

Yes, this recipe has a ton of spices in it, but that's how I like it. In fact, it's scary how much spice we put in this dish. But the flavors complement each other beautifully and make for a rich, aromatic, delicious dish. *Hashweh* is a great side dish for kebabs or any other family meal.

2 tbsp (30 g) olive oil

½ cup (68 g) pine nuts

1 lb (454 g) ground lamb

½ cup (80 g) diced onion

1 garlic clove, smashed

2 tsp (12 g) kosher salt

½ tsp black pepper

2 tsp (4 g) allspice

2 tsp (4 g) cinnamon

½ tsp nutmeg

2 cups (370 g) long-grain rice

4 cups (950 ml) chicken broth

Pinch of saffron

Pour the olive oil in a medium-sized sauce pan (the same pan you will use to cook the rice) over medium-low heat and add the pine nuts. Toast lightly while stirring gently with a wooden spoon, about 45 seconds to 1 minute, then turn the heat up slightly. Stir for another 45 seconds to 1 minute, until the pine nuts turn a light toasted brown color. Scoop out the pine nuts and set aside on paper towels, being careful to leave all the oil behind.

Increase the heat to medium and brown the meat lightly in the same oil, breaking the meat apart finely with a wooden spoon while stirring. Add the onion, garlic, salt and all the spices. Stir in with the meat and sauté about 2 more minutes. Add the rice and mix in with the meat. Sauté until the rice is lightly brown and has absorbed all the fat, stirring occasionally, about 3 to 5 minutes.

Add the broth and saffron and bring to a boil. Give it a good stir. Cover, reduce the heat and simmer about 25 minutes or until the rice absorbs all the liquid. Do not stir the rice while simmering. Remove from the heat and let rest for 10 minutes. Fluff the rice gently with a spoon or fork. Place on a family-style platter. Sprinkle pine nuts on top. Top the platter of rice with your favorite kebabs, or serve as a side with any meat dish.

MUHAMARAH DIP

Muhamarah is thick red bell-pepper paste that my mom used to make back in Beirut, typically as a dip for bread and vegetables or as a topping for beloved Manakish (see page 58). Today I often use it to marinate lamb or duck, a delicacy we never had back home. Sometimes I grill the meat and watch as the red sauce bleeds all over the Mountain-Style Saj Bread (page 56) that we pair it with. It looks great and tastes even better!

1 lb (454 g) red bell peppers

½ cup (63 g) walnuts

3 cloves of garlic

2 tbsp (30 ml) lemon juice

½ cup (120 ml) pomegranate syrup

1 tsp whole cumin, toasted and ground fine

½ cup (15 g) breadcrumbs

2 tsp (4 g) Aleppo pepper

2 tsp (4 g) cayenne pepper (more for spicier flavor)

1 tbsp (18 g) kosher salt

6 oz (180 ml) olive oil

Roast the whole bell peppers on top of a gas stovetop fire or in a grill fire until black and blistered on all sides. Place the peppers in paper bag and seal the top for about 30 minutes to steam them. Remove from the bag, cut in half and remove the stems and seeds. Place the peppers and all the other ingredients except olive oil in a food processor. Puree into a thick paste. Scrape down the sides of food processor with a plastic spatula. Turn the processor back on and slowly add the oil until it is blended well. Serve as a party dip with pita bread, vegetables or kebabs.

MUHAMARAH DUCK KEBABS

My buddy Bob Ambrose owns Bella Bella Gourmet in Connecticut, which represents a group of farmers in New York who raise the best ducks and produce the tastiest foie gras in the United States. I suggest using their duck breast for this dish if you have access to it. Otherwise, use the highest quality duck you can find.

2 to 3 lb (908 to 1362 g) boneless duck breasts, cut into 1¼-inch (3-cm) cubes

Muhamarah Dip (page 50)

Marinate the cubed breast meat in half a serving of muhamarah dip overnight in a resealable bag. Heat the grill to very hot. Place 5 to 6 pieces of duck on steel skewers or bamboo skewers that have been soaked at least 1 hour. Cook the duck 2 to 3 minutes per side. Do not overcook, as duck will get tough and chewy. Serve rare to medium rare. Garnish with the remaining muhamarah dip and serve with pita bread, Mountain-Style Saj Bread (page 56) or Manakish (page 58).

HOMESTYLE LABNEH (GOAT MILK CHEESE)

MAKES ABOUT 12 LABNEH BALLS

Labneh is a cheese spread you find in every home in Lebanon. It's always jarred in olive oil and looks fantastic sitting on the kitchen counter or shelf. It's a great addition to a charcuterie plate or party platter and tastes delicious spread on bread and especially when served beside my Chicken Liver Pâté (page 42).

1 gallon (3.8 L) goat's milk

2 to 3 tbsp (30 to 45 ml) Greek yogurt with live culture

2 tbsp (36 g) kosher salt

Olive oil

Stir milk constantly in large pot over medium heat until it starts simmering and bubbles gently. Pay very close attention so that the milk does not scald or burn. Turn off the heat. Let the milk cool slightly to between 110 and 115°F (43 to 46°C). It is cool enough when you can insert your finger in the milk for 10 seconds without burning it, but no longer than that. Stir in the yogurt. Cover the pot tightly with a lid then wrap it in heavy towels to contain the heat so that the milk cools very slowly. Let sit for 24 hours. Do not open or touch the pot. The next day, refrigerate the mixture for 24 hours.

At this point, the milk should be the texture of creamy yogurt. Stir in the kosher salt. Place the entire mixture in a large cheesecloth. A very clean pillowcase is a good home-style substitute. Push out all the liquid by squeezing the cheese and twisting the cloth into a tight ball. Squeeze out as much liquid as possible, but don't push so hard that the curds come out. Then tie up the cloth tightly and hang in a cool, dry place for 24 to 36 hours. The cheese should develop a nice, creamy texture. Taste and season with more salt if desired. Oil hands lightly then roll up pieces of the cheese into small spheres, about the size of a golf ball. Pour olive oil into a mason jar until it's about ¼ filled. Add the labneh balls until jar is lightly packed. Top with more oil. Serve on top of Mountain-Style Saj Bread (page 56) or crostini or as part of a charcuterie plate or party platter with meats and cheeses.

FASOULIA
(LEBANESE LAMB SHANK AND WHITE BEAN STEW)

SERVES 4 TO 6

Beans were essential to our diet in Lebanon, where meat was scarce. We might have had chicken on Sundays and grilled meat on holidays or specials occasions. That was it. So beans were a critical source of protein. Typically, we'd come home to find a stew of beans and rice in a pot on the stove. That was dinner. Rice and bean stew, known as *fasoulia* in Lebanon, though there are similar versions around the Mediterranean. I loved meat, even then as a kid. So I hated the stew. But as I got older and became a professional cook, I began to appreciate this important piece of my culinary heritage and began to appreciate the efforts my mom made to feed her family with limited means amid trying circumstances. So in deference to my culinary past I began to make my own fasoulia in recent years—but always with meat!

1 cup (208 g) dry white beans (navy, cannellini or broad beans)

Salt and pepper to taste

2 lamb shanks, about 1 lb (454 g) each

3 tbsp (45 ml) olive oil

1 large onion, diced

1 celery rib, chopped diagonally

2 carrots, chopped diagonally

3 cloves garlic, crushed

1 (14.5-oz [428-ml]) can diced tomatoes with liquid

2 oz (56 g) tomato paste

4 cups (950 ml) chicken or beef stock

1 tsp cinnamon, ground

2 cinnamon sticks

1 tsp allspice

1 tsp Aleppo pepper

½ tsp nutmeg

2 bay leaves

Soak the beans overnight in salted water. Salt and pepper the shanks well then pour oil into a heavy, medium-sized pot over medium-high heat. Sear the shanks until browned and well colored on all sides, about 6 to 8 minutes. Set the meat aside.

Add the onion, celery, carrots and garlic and sauté, stirring occasionally, until the onion and garlic are well browned. Add to the pot the diced tomatoes, paste, stock, cinnamon, allspice, Aleppo pepper, nutmeg and bay leaves. Stir well to combine. Add more salt if desired. Bring to a boil, add the shanks, then cover the pot and reduce the heat to simmer for 1 hour. Stir and turn shanks occasionally. After 1 hour, drain the beans and stir into the pot. Simmer another 60 to 70 minutes until the beans are soft, but not broken down to mush. Remove the shanks and let cool about 15 minutes. Shred the meat by hand, being careful to remove any bone or cartilage. Remove the bay leaves and cinnamon sticks and return the meat to the pot. Stir together. Serve in a bowl with crusty bread.

SAJ BREAD AND OUR ESCAPE TO THE LEBANON MOUNTAINS

The violence in Beirut eventually got so bad that living in the city was no longer an option. We escaped to Maasser El Chouf, a village in the Lebanon mountains that surround the city. While there I went to a small Christian school for the year and we lived with my maternal grandmother, Outtor.

It's snowy and cold in these mountains and woods. But the once vast forests of the famous cedars of Lebanon are now scarce. So the people there created an innovative way to cook bread with a minimal amount of fuel. It's called saj bread, and I loved it. Still do.

They build a small fire, and then place a sheet of very thin, rounded metal over the fire—almost like a large wok turned upside down. The metal heats up quickly. Then they lay the dough over the hot metal and bake it on one or both sides. Instant bread!

My grandmother made saj once a week, maybe 100 loaves at a time. She worked the dough into these huge circles of almost paper-thin consistency and nobody did it better. Not everyone has that kind of hard-earned skill, though, including me. So my saj is a bit thicker, smaller and easier to make, but still just as delicious.

The beauty of saj bread is that you can cook it almost anywhere: in your kitchen, on a grill or even over a campfire. A wok turned upside down over a gas-fired stove top is actually the perfect platform to cook saj bread. That's how I cook it today. Saj is also incredibly versatile. You can flavor it almost any way possible, kind of like pizza. The only limit is your imagination. Some of my favorite ways to cook saj bread are found here.

MOUNTAIN-STYLE SAJ BREAD

MAKES ABOUT 10 TO 12 LOAVES

2 tsp (8 g) active dry yeast

2¼ cups (540 ml) warm water (about 110 to 115°F [43 to 46°C]), divided

1 tsp sugar

5 cups (625 g) all-purpose flour

1 tsp salt

2 tbsp (30 ml) olive oil, plus additional oil for coating dough

Mix the yeast in ¼ cup (60 ml) warm water. Add the sugar and let stand for 10 minutes. Sift the flour and salt into a warm bowl. Mix in the oil and rub the oil into the flour with your fingertips, ensuring the oil is spread evenly throughout the flour. Form a well in the center of the flour. Pour in the yeast mixture and remaining warm water. Begin to mix by hand. Add additional flour if the dough is too moist. Turn out dough onto a floured surface and knead about 10 minutes, until smooth and no longer sticky.

Lightly oil a large bowl; place the dough in the bowl and turn to coat it with oil. Cover with a damp cloth and put it in a warm place free of drafts for 1½ to 2 hours. Dough should double in size. Knead for a few minutes then divide into balls about 4 to 5 ounces (112 to 140 g) in weight. Roll the balls into circles on a lightly floured surface with a floured rolling pin, or flatten into in very thin 6- to 8-inch (15- to 20-cm) circles with your hands.

Place wok upside down over a low fire until it is very hot. A cheap, thin wok works best. Oil the bottom of the wok lightly with cooking spray. Flip the flattened dough on the bottom surface of the wok. Cook about 1 minute and then flip to cook the other side. Stack the sheets of bread and cover to keep warm, or serve immediately.

Gently place the saj dough over a wok placed upside-down.

The saj bread will cook through quickly.

Saj is served with different toppings, such as delicious za'atar.

ZA'ATAR SAJ

Za'atar is a spice mixture essential to the Middle Eastern diet. Every home has some on hand and every person, every region, has a preference for the best way to make it. Generally speaking, za'atar is a mix of dried herbs, sesame, salt and sumac. You can purchase za'atar in bulk at the local Middle Eastern market. But I like to mix my own from scratch because I want the sesame seeds toasted to the perfect light brown nuttiness and because I like to accentuate the bright citrus character of high-quality sumac. Mix a bowl of za'atar with a little olive oil and you have a perfect dip or side for sandwiches. Or sprinkle the spice mixture on cheese, sandwiches, even a fresh slice of watermelon.

¼ cup (36 g) sesame seeds

½ cup (22 g) dried thyme

¼ cup (40 g) sumac

2 tsp (12 g) kosher salt

1 tsp ground cumin

⅔ cup (160 ml) extra virgin olive oil

4 to 6 saj loaves

Toast the sesame seeds lightly in a dry skillet over medium heat until the seeds start to brown very lightly, about 3 to 5 minutes. Once the seeds start to brown, remove them from the pan immediately and pour into medium bowl to stop the cooking process. Set the seeds aside. Put thyme, sumac, salt and cumin in a food processor. Blend until the thyme turns powdery. Pour the mixture into the bowl with the toasted sesame seeds. Stir together.

Pour the za'atar spice mixture into a small bowl. Whisk in the oil until well incorporated. Dollop onto the saj bread, spaced equally around the dough to make it easier to spread. Then spread into a thin even layer around the dough with your fingers. Cook the saj on a hot, lightly oiled upside-down wok as directed in the Mountain-Style Saj Bread recipe (page 56), but do not flip. The saj is done when the edges begin to brown and the oil in the za'atar mix begins to bubble. Remove from the heat. Let cool slightly and cut the saj into wedges like you would a pizza.

MANAKISH (LEBANESE FLATBREAD)

MAKES ABOUT 10 TO 12 MANAKISH LOAVES

Manakish is similar to saj in that it's a flatbread that can be topped in a variety of ways. There are two major differences, though. First, manakish is baked in the oven, so it's a little easier to prepare than saj, which is a challenge to get just right even for experienced cooks. And second, manakish is actually much more popular than saj in Lebanon and in other Middle Eastern cultures.

The dough recipe is the same exact recipe used to make saj. But it's prepared slightly differently and cooked differently as well. Namely, you want to create little grooved indents in the surface of the manakish dough with your fingertips while adding your za'atar spread or other toppings. These indents prevent the dough from bubbling up when in the hot oven. They also create an attractive eye-catching texture to the flatbread and they hold pockets of flavor when you're eating your favorite manakish.

Feel free to make manakish dough ahead of time. Then simply cover each piece in plastic wrap and refrigerate up to several days. When you're ready to prepare a meal, simply take the dough out of the refrigerator and top as desired.

2 tsp (8 g) active dry yeast

2 cups (480 ml) warm water (about 110 to 115°F [43 to 46°C])

1 tsp sugar

5¼ cups (656 g) all-purpose flour, divided

1 tsp (6 g) salt

2 tbsp (30 ml) olive oil, plus additional oil for coating dough

Mix the yeast in ¼ cup (60 ml) of warm water. Add the sugar and let stand for 10 minutes. Sift 5 cups (625 g) of flour and the salt into a warm bowl, reserving the additional ¼ cup (60 ml) of flour. Mix in the oil and rub it into the flour with your fingertips, ensuring the oil is mixed evenly throughout the flour. Form a well in the center of the flour. Pour in the yeast mixture and remaining warm water. Begin to mix by hand. If needed, add reserved flour, a spoonful at a time, until the dough is smooth and no longer sticky. Use more flour if needed. Turn out the dough onto a floured surface and knead about 10 minutes, until smooth.

Lightly oil a large bowl, place the dough in the bowl and turn to coat with oil. Cover with a damp cloth and put in a warm place free of drafts for 1½ to 2 hours. Dough should double in size. Push down the dough, and knead for a few more minutes. Divide into about 10 to 12 individual pieces weighing about 4 ounces (112 g) each. Shape each piece of dough into a ball by stretching out the top with your hands and squeezing the sides to push the dough up into a smooth ball shape, following this step several times. Place the dough balls on a sheet pan. Brush each with a little olive oil. Cover with plastic wrap and refrigerate for at least 10 hours or overnight.

Remove the dough from the refrigerator and let it rise to room temperature, at least 45 to 60 minutes. Stretch the balls of dough into small circles on a lightly floured surface with floured hands, then flatten with a floured rolling pin into flattened circles 6 to 8 inches (15 to 20 cm) in diameter.

Preheat oven to 500°F (260°C). Put a pizza stone in the oven, or use an upside-down sheet pan or cookie sheet as a cooking surface. Place manakish dough on a floured pizza peel or upside-down sheet pan. Shake the peel or pan slightly to ensure the dough will slide off into the oven.

Top the manakish dough as desired and, using the tips of your fingers, push small circular indents all over the top of the dough, in the traditional style. As noted, these indents help the dough cook without bubbling, create an attractive texture and help create pockets of flavor in the manakish. Slide the manakish onto the pizza stone in the oven. Bake 5 to 6 minutes each or until edges of the dough turn attractive light brown.

ZA'ATAR MANAKISH WITH LEBANESE SLAW

I first created this slaw years ago for *Guy's Big Bite* on the Food Network. Lebanese slaw is not a real dish back home, just my term to describe the mix of thinly sliced vegetables and chopped herbs I use to make this delicious and healthy version of manakish. The mint adds great aroma, the lemon brightens up the whole dish and the za'atar brings it all together with traditional flavor. The za'atar tastes so good with all those vegetables, it's really one of my favorites.

Zest and juice of 2 lemons

¼ cup (60 ml) extra-virgin olive oil

1 tsp salt

1½ tsp (3 g) Aleppo pepper or red pepper flakes

2 cups (95 g) romaine lettuce, finely sliced

½ small red onion, finely sliced

½ red pepper, seeded, julienned

½ English cucumber, peeled and diced

1 cup (240 g) cherry tomatoes, halved

¼ cup (15 g) coarsely chopped flat leaf parsley

2 tbsp (2 g) chopped fresh mint leaves

1 cup (112 g) Za'atar Saj (page 57)

6 Manakish (page 58)

Preheat your oven to 500°F (260°C). Combine the lemon zest and juice, olive oil, salt and pepper in a small bowl. Whisk well and set aside. In a medium mixing bowl add the romaine, red onion, red pepper, cucumber, cherry tomatoes, parsley and mint. Mix together until well combined. Pour lemon dressing over the slaw. Toss to thoroughly coat, being careful not to bruise the lettuce. Spread the za'atar spread evenly over each manakish with your fingers. Bake 5 to 6 minutes. Spread slaw evenly among each manakish. Roll like a burrito and slice into individual servings, or keep flat and slice like a pizza pie.

LAHME BI AJEEN MANAKISH (LEBANESE MEAT PIE)

Lahme bi ajeen is a savory and luxurious meat stew on manakish traditionally served for breakfast. In my family we'll eat it any time of day. I typically make lahme bi ajeen in the morning, but then keep it around all day in the refrigerator. Sometimes I'll throw a couple lahme bi ajeen in the oven for a quick night-time snack while watching the Red Sox.

1 lb (454 g) ripe red tomatoes, not roma, diced very fine

1 medium onion, diced very fine

2 cloves garlic, smashed into paste

2 tbsp (32 g) pepper paste (substitute with tomato paste if desired)

2 tsp (4 g) ground cinnamon

2 tsp (4 g) ground cumin

2 tsp (4 g) paprika

2 tsp (4 g) cayenne

1 tsp pomegranate syrup

1 tsp black pepper

1 tbsp (18 g) kosher salt, plus more to garnish

1 lb (454 g) finely ground beef (80/20 mix) or finely ground fatty lamb

6 Manakish (page 58)

Lemon juice

Preheat the oven to 500°F (260°C). Put a pizza stone in the oven, or simply use an upside-down sheet pan or cookie sheet. Mix together all the ingredients, except the beef or lamb, manakish and lemon, in a large bowl. The mixture should be on the wet side and bright red. Add the meat and mix together well. Top the manakish dough with about ½ cup (120 g) of the mixture and spread into a thin layer with your fingers. Bake 7 to 8 minutes. Garnish with kosher salt and fresh-squeezed lemon juice.

Note: It's important the meat is finely ground, more finely ground than typical hamburger meat, to give these manakish the right texture. Ask your butcher for fine-ground meat before making this recipe.

CHEESE MANAKISH

This is really a quick and easy manakish, but no less delicious than the rest. My favorite cheese manakish are made with a mix of mozzarella and feta but, in reality, you can use any cheese you want. You can also garnish this version of Lebanese flatbread many different ways. Try some chopped cucumber and torn mint for a pretty presentation, or even a bit of my own Lebanese Slaw (see page 60).

1 cup (112 g) shredded whole-milk mozzarella

1 cup (150 g) crumbled feta cheese

2 tbsp (28 g) unsalted butter, melted

2 tsp (4 g) Aleppo pepper or 1 tsp fresh-cracked black pepper

6 Manakish (page 58)

Mix the cheese, butter and pepper together well. Spread over manakish dough in a thin, even layer, leaving a crust edge of about ½ inch (12 mm) in width. Bake at 500°F (260°C) for 7 to 8 minutes.

HOMEMADE GHEE

MAKES ABOUT 1 CUP (240 ML)

Ghee is little more than clarified butter, the way it's usually prepared in the Middle East. I grew up watching my mom make a big batch of ghee every month or two. I always have some on hand and use it for almost any recipe that calls for butter or clarified butter. It gives me the comfy feeling of being home with my mother.

1 lb (450 g) butter

Cut the butter into cubes and place in a saucepan. Heat the butter over medium heat until completely melted. Reduce to a simmer. Cook about 10 to 15 minutes. During this time, the butter will go through several stages. It will foam, then bubble, then seem to almost stop bubbling and then foam again. When the second foam occurs the ghee is done. At this point, the melted butter should be bright gold in color and there should be reddish brown pieces of milk solids at the bottom of the pan.

Let cool slightly for 2 to 3 minutes and then slowly pour through a wire mesh strainer lined with several layers of cheesecloth. Discard solids. Ghee will last up to a month at room temperature or even longer in refrigerator. Use as a substitute for oil when pan-searing or sautéing food.

CHAPTER 3

Melting Pot Mainstays

The violence in Lebanon finally got unbearable by the summer of 1978, both in the streets of Beirut and in the mountains. Much of the city was shelled and destroyed. People were slaughtered in the mountain villages. So many people died, often gruesome deaths, and even more people were left homeless. My dad's relatives were killed in one massacre; my mom's relatives in another, including my uncle George and my grandmother Outtor, whom we had lived with there in the mountains.

It was time to get out.

We fled to America, but our goal was to return home when the war ended. Of course, the war raged until 1990. And by then our lives were fully wrapped up in America, in being American and in being thankful for all the opportunities afforded to us by life in the United States.

But life here didn't start out so great. In fact, the move to Boston was the toughest time of my life. We settled into a triple-decker in Boston's blue-collar Roslindale neighborhood—"Rozzy" as it's known locally. I had no friends and I couldn't speak English—my struggles to learn a new language were compounded, I later learned, by dyslexia. Even worse, I got my ass kicked every day by all the Irish kids. There were times when I'd get off the school bus and run straight home three or four blocks so I didn't get beat up. I wanted to go back home to Lebanon. War or not. That was my home. My friends were there and they spoke my languages, French and Arabic.

Roslindale, and all of Boston, was changing very fast at the time. It was the late 1970s, not long after the school busing crisis painted Boston as an intolerant, racist town. When I got there, black kids couldn't even walk through Rozzy Square. Arab kids like me didn't have it much better.

There were many positives in these early years in America, though. Despite some trouble here and there, it was nothing like the violence back home. And despite some racial incidents, Boston was and is actually a very diverse, multicultural place with people from many different countries—much like the great melting pot of the United States in general. And that meant a whole new world of amazing food I had never imagined back in Beirut. And the best part: there was plenty of it!

There were days back in Lebanon when you had to walk a mile just to get water. It didn't matter if you were rich or poor. Water itself at times was hard to find, let alone a great variety of bountiful food. Here in Roslindale, we were surrounded by food. Cheap food, plentiful food that a working family like ours could afford; food representing cultures from all over the world. Chinese food. Middle Eastern food. Greek food. Italian food. Especially Greek and Italian food, which could be found everywhere and remain important to me today.

Beirut sits right on the throat of the Mediterranean Sea, but seafood, for whatever reason, was not a big part of our diet there. We would fish quite often in a seaside community called Jounieh, right there on the Mediterranean. But we enjoyed only a few different ways of making fish, basically fried or baked whole. At least I didn't know much about different kinds of seafood, and we lived only a short distance from the sea. Here in Boston, with its long fishing history built upon cod, lobster and shellfish, seafood is a huge part of the diet. In fact, Boston, for my money, is still the best place in the world to eat seafood.

My dad would take my brothers and me down to Castle Island, a famous old colonial fort on the South Boston waterfront that is a very popular recreation area. It was such a big deal, it was like a vacation for us. We'd throw a couple lines in the water, and we'd never fail to fill a big bucket with flounder, right there on Boston Harbor. It was amazing! The abundance of fish seemed so new and fresh and novel to me, on top of all the various ethnic cuisines right in my own neighborhood. You could find and eat just about anything in Roslindale and I loved it all!

By the time I had turned 14 years old, life in America had improved dramatically.

First, I had bulked up and toughened up, thanks to a local restaurateur and former pro boxer named Vinny Marino, who encouraged me to join his boxing gym. I loved boxing and got good at it real fast. I lifted weights, trained almost every day and learned some martial arts, too. Plus, it got me off the streets. Kids were no longer trying to pick on me—and if they did, they got the beating, not me.

Second, Vinny got me a job working at his eponymous Italian restaurant, Vinny Marino's. Classic red sauce Italian-American joint. Ironically, it was at one point a restaurant called Casa Beirut. I started out washing dishes for him. Before long I was working the line. I learned to master all the classics of Italian-American dining: chicken Parmesan, chicken piccata, meatballs, shrimp scampi. Moving to Boston introduced me to a whole new world of food; now I was learning to cook a new world of food, too.

Vinny took a liking to me and called me "the Mayor." I learned only recently that he called me the Mayor because he thought that I acted like I owned the town as a teenager. In reality, Vinny was the real mayor of Roslindale. He was the type of guy who always dressed nice, drove a big-ass shiny black car and seemed to know everybody. He always had money in his pocket and was always helping the neighborhood. I envied him. Even as a boy I remember thinking, "I want to be like Vinny someday." I wanted to own a restaurant and have a few bucks in my pocket and be seen as a guy who made his neighborhood better. Vinny became my first American role model, a man who represented all the opportunity the United States afforded people from all different backgrounds, provided they wanted to work hard.

Vinny told me many years later as an adult that he took me under his wing because he felt a kinship with the struggles I faced as a foreign kid in a new country. Vinny, you see, was a boy during World War II, at a time when Italians were persecuted because we were fighting Italy in the war and American boys, boys from right here in Roslindale, were getting killed over there. He got picked on a lot and got into a lot of fights—just like what happened to me. Vinny ultimately toughened up and became a very successful boxer. He helped me toughen up, too. He taught me a lot.

Vinny is still a friend today, more than 30 years later, and he's still in the restaurant business. He owns the Brickhouse Café in Dedham and his meatballs are the best I've ever had. I still have a strong affinity for Italian-American food. Some of the best Italian in Greater Boston today is also in Dedham, at Vincenzo's Italian Specialty Store and Deli. Owner Giuseppe "Joe" Musto is my go-to guy for great Old World Italian.

My Americanization continued as I started to hang out with a great group of friends from all different backgrounds, including my pal Billy Papadopoulos, a Greek immigrant kid who was running his family's pizza joint at age 14. Billy is a big teddy bear today. But when we were teenagers he was big and tough and naturally strong. If anyone was going to mess with me, they had to go through Billy, too. Most kids were smart enough not to mess with us.

We hung with a pretty tough crew and, like many teenage boys, the temptations on the street started to call. If we weren't in the kitchen we were usually in trouble. We got into a lot of fights, we looked for them actually, and plenty of other teenage trouble: racing cars, mouthing off to teachers, some petty crimes. I got kicked out of Catholic Memorial, a very prestigious high school in Boston. And, in fact, I never finished high school at all—a reality that has embarrassed me for many years. But I was tough, and I wanted everybody to know it. The cops got to know me, too. Jail looked like a very real possibility in the not too distant future.

I had one thing going for me and one thing only: a love of food and a rapidly developing foundation in cooking. Billy's parents Taso and Angela owned a pizza shop in Boston's Brighton neighborhood, Center House of Pizza. But they didn't speak a word of English. So Billy basically ran the place as a teenager.

He'd head over there after school and work until closing at 11 p.m. I helped him most nights. The place was slammed and we worked our asses off making pizza—thick, craggy-crust pan pizza in the Greek style. People loved it! We learned a lot about customer service, keeping people happy, doing business and hustling for a dollar. Two immigrant kids learning to carve out their own destiny in the Land of Opportunity with a little hard work and initiative.

Billy is still the best pizza maker I know. Today he owns Ultimate Pizza in the suburban Boston community of Easton, where he specializes in what's known around Greater Boston as bar pizza or pub pizza—essentially, an evolution of Greek pan pizza cooked in steel pans, served in 10-inch (25-cm) personal sizes and popular at local watering holes, especially south of the city. Some folks around Boston call it South Shore–style pizza, but it definitely has its roots in Greek-American tradition.

Billy's pizza is awesome. But the dish I loved most was Billy's mom's souvlaki. It was fantastic! They'd cook it over charcoals at family parties. But we developed our own version that we cooked in the pizza shop to feed ourselves at the end of a long night. Instead of grilling lamb or pork on skewers with some vegetables, we cut the meat into strips and sautéed it with julienned peppers and onions—then finished it with some lemon juice and tzatziki sauce.

We'd even throw some pizza dough in the oven and make fresh pita bread, too. And on a really good night, we'd sneak into Billy's dad's stash of ouzo and wash down our homemade souvlaki with a couple stiff drinks. It was just like being in Greece—but right here in Boston!

My knowledge of food during the first years of my life was limited to the simple Mediterranean and Middle Eastern dishes of Lebanon. Here in Boston, in the space of a few years, I'd already learned to enjoy and cook American bar food, New England classics, Italian-American fare and the staples of a Greek diet. My concept of food was changing rapidly and I loved it all. I couldn't wait to learn more!

GUINNESS BEEF STEW, STRAIGHT FROM THE DUBLIN BREWERY

SERVES 4

The Irish are still Boston's predominant ethnicity. Plenty of Irish immigrants live here and we have the beloved Boston Celtics, a great St. Patrick's Day Parade and an Irish pub on every corner, including in my old Roslindale neighborhood. Every Boston mayor for more than 100 years, except for my late pal Mayor Tom Menino, was an Irishman.

Of course, as I said earlier, my first encounters with the Boston Irish did not go well. I got into a lot of fights with the Irish kids back in the 1970s and 1980s, a rough-and-tumble time for the city. Eventually, though, I made a lot of Irish friends, and I even married into a big Irish-American family.

I finally visited Ireland for the first time in 2016, where I met Justin O'Connor, the executive chef for the 1837 Bar & Brasserie, right inside the Guinness brewery. It's a beautiful restaurant in an old reclaimed corner of this massive and world-famous brewery, which is one of the top tourist attractions in all of Europe. We tried his Guinness beef stew and it was delicious. You can find Guinness beef stew in almost every corner of Boston, but I wanted a recipe straight from the source, straight from Ireland, and Chef Justin was kind enough to share.

8 oz (240 ml) Guinness Foreign Extra Stout, divided

2 tbsp (28 g) butter

1 lb (454 g) stewing beef, diced

1 medium onion, diced

1 large carrot, diced

1 large celery stalk, diced

1 large parsnip, diced

2 large potatoes, diced

4 cups (950 ml) thickened beef stock

Sprigs of fresh thyme & rosemary

Marinate the beef for 24 hours in half the Guinness. Preheat the oven to 350°F (176°C). Melt the butter and brown the beef well on the stovetop in a heavy, oven-safe stew pot. Add the onion, carrot, celery, parsnip and potato and sauté 4 to 5 minutes. Add the beef stock, herbs and remaining Guinness. Cover the pot and roast in the oven, stirring occasionally, for 90 minutes, or until the beef is tender. Ladle the stew into four bowls and serve with creamy mashed potatoes if desired.

BOSTON MAPLE-WHISKEY STEAK TIPS

SERVES 4

The first time I had steak tips, probably at about 11 or 12 years old, was something of a life-changing experience given the scarcity of meat of any kind, especially beef, back home in Beirut. Steak tips are a kind of Boston specialty you find at take-out joints and pubs all over the city.

Steak tips come from the thin but fatty-rich sirloin flap, typically a chewy, second-rate cut of meat. So the beef is cut into chunks, marinated to flavor and tenderize the beef, then grilled over a hot fire. Sometimes the tips are skewered, but more often than not they're just piled onto a plate, maybe doused with barbecue sauce, and served with French fries. Meat was something you ate back in Lebanon only on special occasions. Here in America, you could walk into a little takeout joint like my buddy Billy's family pizza shop and walk out with a pile of grilled marinated beef for just a few dollars. I was amazed by it all.

2 lb (908 g) sirloin flap or flatiron steak

½ cup (120 ml) South Boston Irish Whiskey (or favorite whiskey)

¼ cup (60 ml) Grade B Massachusetts maple syrup (or favorite real maple syrup)

¼ cup (60 ml) soy sauce

1 tbsp (15 ml) Dijon mustard

1 tbsp (15 ml) Worcestershire sauce

2 tbsp (25 g) brown sugar

2 tbsp (20 g) finely chopped shallots

1 tsp garlic powder

1 medium onion, chopped into large pieces

Cut the meat into 2-inch (5-cm) chunks. Whisk together all the remaining ingredients. Pour the liquid into a large resealable bag. Add the beef and marinate overnight. Turn the grill to high or build a hot charcoal fire. Grill the tips about 3 minutes per side for medium-well. The best tips have charred edges. Steak tips are, by definition, not the highest quality cut of meat, so they taste better to me cooked a little beyond medium. Pour your favorite supermarket barbecue sauce over the tips if desired and serve with rice, French fries or salad. I also like to serve my steak tips with an onion that's been quartered, dabbed with a little olive oil and grilled beside the steak tips until lightly charred.

NEW ENGLAND-STYLE OYSTER BISQUE

Oysters were essential to the American diet in the early days of the country here in Boston and in other coastal communities. Oysters were largely overfished through the centuries, but have enjoyed an incredible revival in recent years. We now have small farmers all over the Massachusetts coast growing and selling beautiful oysters and serving them at the best restaurants here in Boston and in other cities around the country. New England, for my money, grows the best oysters in the world. The cold water keeps them firm and salty and delicious. There's nothing better than shucking and sucking down some delicious salty, cold-water New England oysters—except maybe working them into this rich, savory bisque.

1 lb (454 g) shucked oysters, with reserved brine

8 tbsp (112 g) butter, divided

1½ cups (240 g) diced white onion

1 cup (100 g) diced celery

1 tsp salt, or to taste

½ tsp white pepper, or to taste

¼ tsp dried thyme

3 cloves garlic, mashed

¼ cup (31 g) all-purpose flour

1 cup (240 ml) dry white wine

¼ tsp ground nutmeg

2½ cups (600 ml) bottled clam juice

2 cups (480 ml) cream

Rinse and scrub the oyster shells before shucking to remove any loose shell or other debris. Carefully reserve the brine from each oyster. Strain the brine through a fine-mesh sieve into a sauce pot. Toss out any shell pieces left behind.

Melt 4 tablespoons (56 g) of butter in a medium-sized pot over medium heat. Add the onion and celery and season with salt and pepper. Sauté until the onion and celery are just translucent, about 2 to 4 minutes. Do not let the onion brown. Add the thyme and garlic. Sauté 1 minute until the garlic is fragrant. Add the flour slowly and stir constantly for 2 minutes to create a roux. Add the wine and nutmeg. Mix well, stirring for about 2 to 3 minutes to allow the roux to thicken. Add the reserved oyster brine and clam juice and whisk well. Add ¾ of the whole oysters. Simmer about 6 to 7 minutes and during this time roughly chop the remaining oysters.

Remove the stew from the heat and pour carefully into a food processor. Blend until the mixture is completely smooth. You may want to blend in two portions if there is too much stew. Pour the mixture back into the pot. Whisk the cream in slowly. Place the pot over low heat and bring to a very low simmer. Add the remaining chopped oysters. Simmer 7 to 8 minutes, until the oysters are cooked through. Make sure the bisque does not boil. Simmer longer for a thicker texture if desired. Check the flavor and season with additional salt and white pepper if desired. Whisk in the remaining 4 tablespoons (56 g) of butter.

"BE PROUDA YA CHOWDA" NEW ENGLAND CLAM CHOWDER

SERVES 6 TO 8

Guy Fieri of Food Network fame discovered Mike's City Diner several years ago and has featured us on his immensely popular show, *Diners, Drive-Ins, and Dives*. We've since become friends and he's been kind enough invite me back on Triple D, as well as *Guy's Big Bite* and *Guy's Grocery Games* many times. I prepared this chowder for an episode of *Guy's Big Bite* called "Be Prouda Ya Chowda." I think it represents Boston well!

5 cups (1185 ml) clam juice

1 lb (454 g) potatoes, diced

5 slices bacon, ½-inch (1.2-cm) dice

1 small yellow onion, diced

3 bay leaves

1 tbsp (1 g) freshly chopped thyme leaves

½ stick (56 g) butter

½ cup (62 g) all-purpose flour

2 cups (480 ml) half and half

2 lb (908 g) freshly shucked clams, roughly chopped

2 tbsp (7 g) chopped fresh parsley leaves

Kosher salt and white pepper to taste

Oyster crackers, to serve

Black pepper, to serve

Bring the clam juice and potatoes to a boil in a large soup pot. Cook until the potatoes are tender, about 10 minutes. Set aside. In a separate pot, prepare a roux by rendering the bacon until crispy. Stir in the onion and sauté until translucent, about 6 to 8 minutes. Add the bay leaves, thyme and butter and let the butter melt. Reduce heat to low. Whisk in the flour and cook until a golden brown roux forms, about 3 to 4 minutes, stirring constantly so as not to burn the roux.

Bring the clam juice and potato back to a boil. Whisk a ladleful of clam juice into the roux then gradually whisk the roux back into the soup pot until it thickens. Slowly whisk in the half and half and reduce the heat to a simmer while whisking. Add the clams and simmer 2 to 3 minutes to cook through. Add the parsley and salt and pepper to taste. Serve hot with oyster crackers. Garnish each bowl with a dash of fresh-cracked black pepper.

LOCKE-OBER'S LOBSTER SAVANNAH

SERVES 2 TO 4

Lobster is New England's signature seafood, the one most people associate with Boston and the region in general. I never ate lobster until arriving in Boston, where almost every restaurant serves it in some capacity—whether the casual seafood shanty lobster roll or rich and decadent fine-dining lobster Savannah.

Lobster Savannah was the signature recipe of the former Locke-Ober restaurant in Boston's Downtown Crossing, for over 100 years the city's most famous dining landmark. About 35 years after arriving in Boston as a boy from Lebanon, some business partners and I purchased the famous Locke-Ober building on Winter Place. As we walked around the site of the late, great restaurant, I came upon a big folder full of Locke-Ober recipes—including this recipe for its signature lobster Savannah!

We eventually auctioned off much of the equipment, art and furniture left in the building, and before long Locke-Ober was replaced by Yvonne's, a modern supper club that pays tribute to the legacy of the space and has since become a new Boston dining landmark. But I held on to that pile of Locke-Ober recipes for myself—a bit of Boston culinary history right here in my hands.

4 (2-lb [908-g]) lobsters

2 tbsp (28 g) butter

12 large white mushrooms, chopped to ½ inch (12 mm)

3 shallots, finely chopped

½ red bell pepper, chopped to ½ inch (12 mm)

¼ cup (60 ml) brandy

½ cup (120 ml) cream sherry

2 cups (480 ml) heavy cream

Pinch of paprika

Salt and freshly ground black pepper to taste

Juice of half a lemon

¼ cup (25 g) finely grated Parmigiano-Reggiano cheese

Steam the lobsters for 10 minutes. Remove the meat from the claws and knuckles and set aside. With kitchen shears, cut a long wide rectangle out of the top of each body, about 1½ inches (4 cm) wide and about 5 inches (13 cm) long. Keeping the body in one piece, carefully pry the meat from the tail and set aside. Remove any meat from the body cavity, as well as the green tomalley and set aside. Rinse the lobster bodies and reserve.

Preheat the oven to 400°F (204°C). Cut the lobster meat into 1-inch (2.5-cm) chunks, and set aside in a bowl with the tomalley. Place a large sauté pan over high heat and melt the butter. Add the mushrooms, and stir until they begin to release their juices, about 1 to 2 minutes. Add the shallots and red pepper, and stir until the liquid has evaporated and the shallot is translucent, about 5 to 8 minutes.

Remove the pan from the heat and add the brandy and sherry. Carefully touch a lighted match to the mixture to flame it. When the flame subsides, place a pan over medium-high heat. Add the heavy cream, paprika and salt and pepper to taste. Add the lobster meat and tomalley to the pan and stir. Add the lemon juice and adjust the seasonings to taste. Allow the sauce to simmer until the lobster is heated and the sauce is slightly thickened, about 5 minutes.

Place the reserved lobster bodies in a large baking pan. Place equal portions of the lobster mixture in the cavities of the bodies, and sprinkle with the cheese. Bake until the cheese is lightly browned, 2 to 3 minutes. Serve immediately.

BILLY'S PORK SOUVLAKI WITH TZATZIKI SAUCE

SERVES 2 TO 4

This is the same pork souvlaki Billy and I cooked as teenagers in his parent's pizza shop in Brighton. It's still the way I cook souvlaki today.

TZATZIKI SAUCE

1½ cups (360 ml) Greek yogurt

½ English cucumber, seeded and finely diced

1 tbsp (15 ml) fresh lemon juice

2 cloves garlic, mashed into paste

2 tbsp (2 g) chopped fresh mint

Salt and pepper to taste

SOUVLAKI

1½ lb (680 g) boneless pork shoulder, cut into ½-inch (1.3-cm) strips 1 to 2 inches (2.5 to 5 cm) long

½ yellow onion, julienned

¼ cup (60 ml) fresh lemon juice

¼ cup (60 ml) olive oil

2 tbsp (30 ml) red wine vinegar

1 tbsp (1 g) fresh oregano, chopped

1 tbsp fresh thyme, chopped

2 cloves garlic, mashed into paste

1 tsp crushed red pepper flakes

Salt and fresh ground black pepper to taste

½ red bell pepper, julienned

Lemon wedges and pita bread, to serve

To make the tzatziki, place paper towels in a large colander or mesh strainer. Pour the yogurt on the paper towels. Let sit for 2 to 3 hours to thicken, either in the refrigerator or at a cool temperature. Mix the yogurt well with all other ingredients by folding gently. You do not want to break the yogurt down, but want to maintain thick consistency. Refrigerate until ready to use.

For the souvlaki, toss all the ingredients except the red bell pepper into a bowl. Marinate for 2 to 3 hours or overnight in the refrigerator.

Heat a large cast-iron pan or griddle to high, until the cooking surface is very, very hot. Pour the mixture in evenly so that it sears quickly. Toss in the julienned pepper. Turn a few times until brown on all sides, about 10 to 11 minutes. Do not overwork the mixture to ensure it browns deeply. Transfer to a plate. Garnish with lemon wedges, warm pita bread and tzatziki sauce.

Tzatziki is a delicious and attractive Greek condiment, best served with warm pita bread and some tradtionally inspired pork souvlaki.

VINNY MARINO'S BRICKHOUSE CAFÉ MEATBALLS

Vinny Marino ultimately sold the Roslindale restaurants where I first learned to cook Italian-American food. He's in his 80s today, still exercises all the time and was recently inducted into the Massachusetts chapter of the Italian-American Sports Hall of Fame for his prowess in the ring back in the day. Vinny's still in the restaurant business, too. The meatballs he serves at the Brickhouse Café in Dedham, Massachusetts, might be the best in Boston.

2½ lb (1.1 kg) 80/20 ground beef

1¼ lb (568 g) ground veal

1¼ lb (568 g) ground pork

1¼ lb (568 g) Romano cheese, grated

¾ lb (340 g) plain fine white bread crumbs

1 cup (60 g) fresh parsley, chopped

6 cloves garlic, chopped

1½ medium white onions, chopped

Salt and pepper to taste

Heavy pinch garlic powder, dry oregano and dry basil

Combine all the ingredients together with an electric mixer until well incorporated. Chill in the refrigerator for about 2 hours. Preheat the oven to 375°F (190°C). Form the mixture into 3-ounce (84-g) balls and place them on a lined cooking sheet. Bake for 35 to 40 minutes. Serve immediately with your favorite marinara, Bolognese or alfredo sauce. Unused meatballs can be refrigerated for several days or frozen for future use.

Note: This recipe makes a great sandwich, too, which we serve at Mike's. Simply place each finished breast on a baguette with a pile of crispy pan-seared pancetta.

CLASSIC ITALIAN-AMERICAN RED SAUCE CHICKEN PARMESAN

SERVES 2 TO 4

It seems everybody loves chicken Parmesan. The kind I grew up making and still make today is fairly traditional. After all, there's no reason to mess with something so delicious: a perfect mixture of crispy chicken, red sauce, cheese and some herbs for color and aroma.

4 skinless, boneless chicken breasts, about 6–8 oz (168–224 g) each

2 tsp (12 g) kosher salt

2 tsp (5 g) fresh cracked black pepper

1 cup (125 g) all-purpose flour

3 eggs, scrambled

2 cups (66 g) panko bread crumbs

2 cups (216 g) plain unseasoned bread crumbs

1 cup (240 ml) olive oil

10 leaves fresh basil, rolled and cut chiffonade

About 1 cup (240 ml) tomato sauce

1 cup (112 g) whole milk mozzarella, shredded

½ cup (50 g) grated Parmesan cheese

Wrap each chicken breast loosely between plastic wrap to prevent splashing and pound flat with a heavy object such as a rolling pin until about ½-inch (12-mm) thick. Season the breasts with salt and pepper. Place the flour in small pan, egg wash next to it in a second pan and bread crumbs, mixed together evenly, in a third pan. Dip a breast in flour, then shake off excess. Dip in the egg mixture, then place in the bread crumbs and make sure the entire chicken breast is coated. Place the breasts side by side on a large plate or flat sheet pan. Let the chicken sit for about 5 minutes, which gives the eggs and bread crumbs some time to bind together and make a better crust. Preheat the oven to 350°F (176°C). Heat the oil in a heavy sauté pan to medium-high. Oil is ready when a couple bread crumbs dropped in the oil sizzle immediately.

Sear the chicken in oil, either one or two breasts at a time, until well browned on both sides, about 1 to 2 minutes per side. If the oil smokes, it is too hot. Place the breasts on a sheet pan. Sprinkle chopped basil on top of each breast. Spoon a thin layer of tomato sauce over each breast. Do not use too much tomato sauce, or the chicken coating will lose its crunchy texture and it will take away from the flavor. Sprinkle mozzarella cheese on the breasts, then sprinkle Parmesan on top. Bake about 10 minutes.

EGGPLANT VARIATION

You can make easy, delicious eggplant Parmesan using the same exact recipe as above. Simply substitute the chicken breasts with ¼-inch (6-mm) thick rounds of fresh eggplant. A typical eggplant will, of course, yield more than four ¼-inch (6-mm) thick slices. You will probably get around 12 slices. The chicken parmesan recipe here should yield enough ingredients to handle all 12 slices.

GIUSEPPE MUSTO'S AMALFI-STYLE PASTA WITH SAUSAGE & BROCCOLI RABE

Vincenzo's Deli in Dedham offers scratch Italian cooking and an Italian sub that is the best sandwich in Boston. I eat it right there standing up at the counter. Owner Giuseppe "Joe" Musto's best dish, though, is his Amalfi-style fusilli with Italian sausage and broccoli rabe. It's incredible savory and filling and, with a little practice, you can whip up a big batch in minutes. It's a great party pleaser!

1 lb (454 g) fusilli pasta

4 to 5 tsp (20 to 25 ml) extra virgin olive oil

¼ cup (20 g) finely chopped white onion

¼ cup (20 g) finely chopped yellow onion

2 cloves garlic, finely chopped

½ cup (120 ml) white wine, divided

¼ lb (113 g) Italian sweet sausage, removed from casing and chopped into bite-sized portions

½ cup (20 g) broccoli rabe

1 cup (122 g) grape tomatoes, halved

1 cup (100 g) grated Parmesan cheese

2 tsp (2 g) chopped parsley

Boil the pasta in salted water to desired texture according to directions. Drain pasta and set aside, but reserve 1 cup (235 ml) of the starchy pasta water. Pour the olive oil in a sauté pan over medium heat. Sauté the onions until they start to turn golden, about 4 to 5 minutes. Add the garlic and sauté until browned, another 3 to 4 minutes. Add about 2 teaspoons (10 ml) of white wine to make the onion and garlic sweat. Stir together gently. Add the sausage and remaining wine. Cook the sausage about 10 minutes, stirring occasionally, until the meat is cooked through. Add pasta to the pan and toss with the sausage for about 2 minutes, then add about half of the reserved starchy water. Add the broccoli rabe, tomatoes and cheese and toss together. The pasta should be moist. If the dish appears too dry, add the remaining starchy water. Garnish with parsley and some more grated cheese if desired.

CHAPTER 4

Falafel Temptations

The temptations of the street came to a dangerous end one night in Boston's Kenmore Square, just outside Fenway Park. It was the night I realized my future was either in a jail or in the kitchen. It was the same night I thought it'd be a good idea to scuffle with a couple cops from Boston University.

There was an old nightclub there called Narcissus. It was an 18+ place with a lot of underage drinking and club drugs. There was always trouble and, at 18 years old, I was always looking for it.

One night it got out of hand—and for no reason, really, other than my own brash, young stupidity. My good buddy Nick Papas, who has since passed away, was driving a car full of our friends when we pulled into the parking lot next to Narcissus. There were a bunch of kids, a lot of girls actually, hanging out in the lot, waiting to go into the club.

For whatever reason, two cops parked in the lot, got out of their car, came over to us and began to hassle Nick. The cops weren't much older than us, maybe 21 or 22, and I thought they were busting Nick's balls just to show off in front of the girls. So I started mouthing off. Next thing you know, they're asking for my license and telling me to get out of the car.

"My license is in my wallet in my back pocket," I snarled at them. "If you want it, try to take it from me."

It was a big mistake—for all of us. They pulled me out of the car and tried to cuff me. I said no fucking way. Keep in mind, at the time, I was always working out, boxing, doing karate. I'd been in a lot of fights against guys bigger than me, and I wasn't afraid of a couple smart-mouth young cops. Next thing you know, the fists were flying and I was trying to punch out two cops in a nightclub parking lot. In fact, I knocked down both of them.

Uh-oh!

Almost instantly, I realized I had messed up. You're an idiot, Jay! You're going to jail. My friends realized I had messed up, too. We might have been tough kids. But we weren't criminals. We were just teenagers who liked to drink and scuffle, like a lot of kids that age. None of us wanted to go to jail and maybe ruin our lives. So my friends grabbed me and tried to cool me off. The cops got up off the ground, cuffed me and threw me in the cruiser.

I still mouthed off to them the whole ride to the station. "Do you know who I am?!" I yelled at them. "Do you know who my father is?!"

There are a lot of rich Middle Eastern students in Boston, especially at Boston University. So maybe they thought I was the son of some rich Arab sheikh or something. I was bluffing, of course. My dad Nicolas was a hard-working guy, but we were nothing special. We were just a blue-collar family from Roslindale.

I'm still shocked to this day that they didn't beat the snot out of me in the back of the cruiser on the side of the road. These were the days back before everyone walking by had a video camera in their pocket. They should have beaten me up, quite frankly. I deserved it. But they didn't lay a hand on me. They actually handled it like most cops do, like professionals. Eventually, the case ended up in court and somehow I walked free. From what I understand, just a few weeks before my incident some BU cops had mistakenly shot or killed a kid at a gas station. The force was under a microscope and—I'm just guessing here—I don't think they wanted the bad publicity that might have come with the case of one kid nearly knocking out two cops in a parking lot, so they dropped the charges.

The judge gave me six months of probation and a stern warning: "You break probation, you will go to jail."

I wasn't a great student in school, but I wasn't dumb. I knew it was time to get my life together, but with the realization I couldn't work for someone else. I had to work for myself, and I had to work in a kitchen. It was the only thing I knew how to do. So, at age 18, I sold my sports car, borrowed a few thousand dollars from my old man and some other family members and bought a little take-out ice cream shop called Temptations Café in Brookline, a very well-to-do community just a couple miles from Roslindale.

I dug deep into my family roots and quickly turned it into a falafel shop. We sold sandwiches, roll ups and all kinds of kebabs: *kofta*, lamb, chicken. It was a small little take-out place, but I was determined to make it authentic. So I made everything from scratch. The falafel, hummus, tabouli, kibbeh, even my own Lebanese dressing, all the classics I had grown up with.

Temptations quickly built a following because we made our food fresh every day. It was healthy, delicious, authentic and there was a market for it. The public loved it! But I didn't.

In fact, Temptations was like a prison sentence. I couldn't afford to get help. I couldn't close down. I was there morning, noon and night, and I still lived with my parents to make ends meet. Even worse: I had lost my license—too many speeding tickets—and couldn't drive. My father would drive me to work each morning. I was a real tough guy, huh? Getting a ride from dad to work each morning. And then, after working 14 or 15 hours, I'd walk to my buddy Teddy Gerontidis's pizza shop in Allston three miles away—a good 45-minute walk—and help him close up for the night and then get a ride with him back to Roslindale.

My falafel shop made little money. But working there, working for myself, shaped my future. Temptations is where I went from street punk to chef and businessman. I refined my cooking, I learned about business, budgeting, banking and, mostly, about dealing with people, with neighbors, vendors and, most importantly, with customers. Some people go to school to learn business. I learned it by living it every day for five years. Mostly I learned that hard work is the foundation of any successful business. If you're not willing to work, if you're not willing to devote every hour of every day to building your business and getting better, don't even bother.

Some people get lucky or are born into money. More power to them. But most of the successful people I know built their business or brand the old-fashioned way, with sweat equity. They hustled before they succeeded. That's how I built Temptations. It was a success at other levels, too. I'm proud to say that Temptations is still alive and well today, long after I sold it. There are several of them located around Brookline and Boston.

One other moment made Temptations the place that changed my life: the day a pretty blonde Irish-American girl walked in the door. Her name was Janet. It was a cold, snowy wintry day and the restaurant was dead. She was like a ray of sunshine in the shop—and in my life.

Janet ordered a falafel sandwich roll up with tahini and my Lebanese salad of cilantro, parsley, tomatoes, lettuce and radish. She also asked for a roll of quarters. My buddy Russell Holmes owned the video store next door and said he knew a girl I needed to meet. The roll of quarters was my clue that this was the girl!

We immediately hit it off, chatting about food and making small talk. She was in school at the time, studying for an exam. I told her if she passed the test, I'd take her out. Well, she passed the test. And, in celebration, we had our first date. Of course, the date wasn't perfect. I had to borrow my friend's car, because I didn't have one. In fact, I still didn't have a license. Thank God for good friends! But I didn't let Janet know at the time that I was driving someone else's car around illegally. I thought she'd never date me again if she found out!

Temptations proved to be the inflection point in my life. It got me off the streets, helped me refine my cooking and taught me solid business principles. I put away some money. And, most importantly, I met Janet. More than 20 years later, we're still together, with four beautiful children and a lovely rural New England home.

Turns out buying Temptations was the best thing I ever did. But selling Temptations was the second best thing I ever did. I had bigger plans in store.

PERFECT FALAFEL WITH TAHINI SAUCE

SERVES 4 TO 6

Like my hummus, this falafel was perfected over many years and countless thousands of batches. I can make these in my sleep. The recipe is pretty straightforward. The tough part is perfecting the "feel" it takes to make the perfect falafel balls in your hands. If you can, try to find a falafel scoop made especially for this purpose. But you'll still need to perfect the feel of getting them right, which comes only with practice. But don't be afraid. Just get after it and make them. Your falafel will taste delicious, even if not perfectly shaped. This falafel is so good it might even change your life. After all, it's the same falafel my future wife Janet ordered the day she first walked into Temptations Café and into my life.

FALAFEL

2 cups (400 g) dried chickpeas

5 cloves garlic

1 large red or yellow onion, diced

1 tbsp (6 g) ground coriander

1 tbsp (6 g) ground cumin

½ tsp cayenne pepper

2 tsp (36 g) kosher salt

1 cup (60 g) finely chopped fresh parsley

1 cup (60 g) finely chopped fresh cilantro

½ cup (120 ml) water

½ tsp baking soda

Oil (peanut, canola or vegetable) for deep-frying

TAHINI SAUCE

1 cup (240 ml) sesame tahini, well shaken

¾ cup (180 ml) cold water

2 cloves garlic, crushed

½ tsp salt or to taste

⅓ cup (80 ml) fresh lemon juice, divided

Pickled Turnip Lebanese-Style (page 144), to serve

Soak the chickpeas overnight in a bowl covered by 3 to 4 inches (8 to 10 cm) of water. The next day, rinse well. Put the chickpeas, garlic, onion, spices, salt, parsley, cilantro and water in a blender. Blend until a smooth consistency, but do not liquefy, about 1 minute. Scrape down the sides with a spatula to ensure the entire mixture is blended evenly and very finely. Pour into a serving bowl. Stir in baking soda 20 minutes before ready to fry.

With a small sorbet scoop, spoon the mixture into wet hands and roll into a meatball-like sphere, no more than ¾ inches (1.9 cm) in diameter, or a slightly flattened sphere of the same size. Mix should be almost spongy and hold together well between your hands. If the mixture doesn't hold together, mix in a small amount of flour to stiffen it. The flour will take away flavor, but that's better than the falafels breaking up when cooking. Roll the entire mixture into falafel balls before frying the first falafel.

In a medium-sized heavy pot, add about 2 to 3 inches (5 to 7.5 cm) of frying oil. Heat to 350°F (176°C) or until a small test piece of the falafel mixture bubbles when added to the oil. Consistent temperature is essential.

Add the falafels slowly into the oil with a slotted spoon. Fry 5 to 6 minutes. After 2 to 3 minutes, move the falafels around to ensure they're not sticking to the bottom of the pan. Place on cookie sheet layered with paper towels to dry.

Put the tahini, water, garlic, salt and half the lemon juice in a food processor. Blend until it's a thick paste, about 2 to 3 minutes. If the paste is too thick, add a little more liquid, either water or lemon juice as desired for taste. If too loose, add 1 tablespoon (15 ml) at a time of additional tahini. It should be the consistency of loose, warm honey.

Serve the falafel with tahini sauce and pickled turnip.

JAY'S ALL-PURPOSE CHICKEN BRINE

I brine almost every piece of poultry I cook, including my signature Thanksgiving Turkey No. 2 (see page 118) and even the chickens I cook day to day for the family. It's very easy, takes little time and adds a lot of flavor.

16 cups (3.8 L) water
½ cup (100 g) sugar
½ cup (144 g) kosher salt
Rind and juice of one lemon

Clean all the chicken before brining to remove any blood. Stir the sugar and salt into the water until dissolved. Stir in the lemon juice. Chop up the rind roughly and add to the brine. Add the chicken. Cure at least 4 hours, but preferably overnight for best flavor. Sixteen cups (3.8 L) of water will brine about 4 to 5 pounds (2 to 2.5 kg) of chicken. Expand measurements proportionately if needed to brine larger amounts of chicken.

MUJADARA (LEBANESE LENTILS & RICE)

SERVES 4

Mujadara is a great and versatile snack or meal when you want to eat light or on the run. It can be served hot, at room temperature or even cold. I like eating it with cucumber salad or Tzatziki Sauce (see page 81).

2 large yellow onions, halved and thinly sliced
¼ cup plus 1 tbsp (75 ml) olive oil, divided
1 large yellow onion, diced
2 cloves garlic, smashed
5 cups (1.1 L ml) water
1½ cups (288 g) dried brown lentils
1 tsp ground allspice
1 tsp ground cumin
½ tsp ground cinnamon
1 tbsp (18 g) kosher salt or to taste
1 cup (185 g) long-grain rice

Slowly caramelize the 2 large sliced onions in ¼ cup (60 ml) olive oil over very low heat for 30 to 40 minutes until richly golden brown, stirring regularly. Set aside.

Heat the remaining tablespoon (15 ml) of oil over medium heat in a medium sauce pot until shimmering. Add the diced onion and sauté until browned, then add the garlic and sauté while stirring, 30 seconds, until fragrant. Add the water and lentils. Turn up the heat and bring the water to a boil. Add the allspice, cumin, cinnamon and salt. Reduce the heat to a simmer. Cover and cook 20 minutes.

Add the rice and stir together well. Cover again and simmer an additional 20 minutes until all liquid is absorbed. Pour the mixture into a bowl or casserole dish and top with the caramelized onions.

FIVE ETERNAL LESSONS ABOUT STARTING A FOOD BUSINESS

Customer service comes first—You might be the best chef in the world. But the customer experience hinges first and foremost on service. A simple smile and a warm hello goes a long way toward making guests feel welcome and quickly sets the stage for a great experience. I made it my mission at Temptations to personally greet every person who walked through the door as if they were my best pal. I didn't have a choice, really. I was the only one there working! But it built a rapport with the neighbors and all my guests and went a long way toward building a good reputation. It's an especially important lesson at new restaurants still working out all the kinks. The guest will forgive a mistake or two in the kitchen and come back again if they enjoy great service and hospitality.

But the customer is not always right—There's a restaurant industry veteran here in Boston named Patrick Maguire who runs a blog called I'm Your Server, Not Your Servant, which works to improve the relationships between guests and service professionals. There are a lot of important lessons in there. The customer is not right, for example, when he mistreats my staff. My employees work hard to deliver a great product and great service. If one of our people makes a mistake or is rude to a guest, I'll deal with it directly and get the problems corrected. I've fired people who mistreated our valuable customers. However, there are guests who feel entitled and simply step out of line and mistreat restaurant staff, too. Those customers are wrong. And they're not welcome back at my restaurant. Simple as that.

Be consistent—Nobody builds a loyal customer base in any business without a consistent product. In the restaurant business, that means if you serve fresh food made from scratch one day, as we did at Temptations, you better make it fresh from scratch again the next day. Loyal customers will know when you've taken a shortcut, and you'll quickly lose their business. I know. I made mistakes early on at Temptations, taking shortcuts when I was lazy or tired. We lost business as a result, and deservedly so. Nobody wants to feel like they are taking a gamble visiting your restaurant. They need to know their favorite item on the menu is going to be just as fresh and delicious tomorrow as it was today.

Be passionate—So many successful businesses start with just one person passionately dedicated to a single goal or idea. The key is passion. Live that business morning, noon and night. You need to know your business inside out, and better than anyone else. Your passion will manifest itself in a better product, while your enthusiasm and dedication will prove contagious to employees, partners and guests.

Stay humble—I don't care how good your food is or how popular your restaurant might become. Nobody likes a jerk. Your livelihood depends on that guest enjoying your food and service, telling friends about the experience and coming back again. Be humble and respectful toward those customers who make your business a success, and they'll treat you well.

MOROCCAN MEATBALLS IN SAFFRON AND LEMON SAUCE

SERVES 6 TO 8

My time at Temptations sparked a renewed interest in the food of my native Lebanon and the rest of the Mediterranean world. I began experimenting with dishes like these Moroccan meatballs, which I've honed and developed over the years. Maybe I'm biased. But this recipe just sounds delicious to me, especially the words "saffron and lemon sauce." You can tell right away it's a gorgeous combination of bright flavors, beautiful colors and delicious, savory mouth feel. I love it. I think your friends and family will love it, too!

MEATBALLS

2 tbsp (12 g) whole cumin

1 yellow onion, chopped

2 cloves garlic, chopped

½ cup (30 g) roughly chopped fresh parsley leaves

1 tsp paprika

1 tsp black pepper

1½ tbsp (27 g) kosher salt

5 slices fresh white supermarket bread, chopped into cubes

3 lb (1362 g) 80/20 mix ground beef or lamb

¼ cup (60 ml) vegetable oil

SAFFRON LEMON SAUCE

4 oz (112 g) Swiss chard, about 4 large leaves

1 onion, chopped fine

3 cloves garlic, minced

2 tbsp (30 ml) vegetable oil

2 tsp (4 g) paprika

1 tbsp (6 g) turmeric

1 tsp cayenne pepper

Salt to taste

½ cup (30 g) roughly chopped fresh parsley, divided

4 cups (950 ml) chicken stock

1 pinch of saffron

½ cup (30 g) roughly chopped cilantro leaves

¼ cup (60 ml) fresh-squeezed lemon juice (about 2 lemons)

For the meatballs, toast the whole cumin for 30 seconds in a hot dry pan, shaking the pan constantly. Cook longer for a darker, stronger, nuttier flavor. Grind the cumin in a spice or coffee grinder. Place the cumin, onion, garlic, parsley, paprika, black pepper and salt in a food processor. When the spices are well ground, slowly add cubes of bread while still grinding. Do not add the bread too fast, or it will bind up the processor. When all the bread has been added, you should have a smooth, liquefied paste.

Mix together the paste and meat with your hands very well until it's bound together like a meatloaf. Refrigerate for 3 to 4 hours or overnight. Roll the mixture into golf-ball-sized meatballs. Heat the vegetable oil in a sauté pan to medium-high until shimmering. Brown the meatballs on all sides, but do not cook through.

To make the sauce, remove the thick bottom stem from each leaf of chard. Fold in half and cut into long strips. Sweat the chard, onion and garlic in vegetable oil over medium-low heat until translucent, about 5 to 6 minutes. Be careful not to burn the garlic. Add the paprika, turmeric, cayenne, salt and half the parsley and stir well. Add the stock and saffron. Bring to a boil, then reduce to a simmer, add the meatballs and cook 45 minutes to 1 hour. When done, add the remaining parsley, cilantro and lemon juice. Stir well. Serve the meatballs in a bowl and garnish with chopped parsley, lemon wedges and crusty bread.

FREEKEH FATTOUSH SALAD

Fattoush is a bold, colorful and multi-textured Middle Eastern salad with vegetables and plenty of herbs mixed with toasted pita bread. It's traditionally dressed with sumac, lemon juice and olive oil. My version is served with *freekeh*, a kind of toasted wheat, instead of pita bread. Freekeh is packed with nutrients and has been touted as the next "supergrain." I ate this salad a lot while training for the Boston Marathon in 2014 and eat it most any time I'm on a diet. It's two very nutritious and delicious tastes that I combine into a single dish. I like the fact that it's a twist on a traditional dish. I also just love the name. Freekeh fattoush! Sounds cool to me.

DRESSING

1 clove garlic plus pinch of salt, smashed into paste

3 tbsp (45 ml) fresh-squeezed lemon juice

⅔ cup (160 ml) extra virgin olive oil

1 tsp sumac

Salt and pepper to taste

FREEKEH

1 tbsp (15 ml) olive oil

1½ cups (270 g) freekeh

3½ cups (830 ml) chicken stock

Pinch of salt and pepper

FOR THE SALAD

1 cup (60 g) roughly chopped Italian parsley

½ cup (30 g) roughly chopped Italian mint

½ cup (30 g) purslane (substitute with watercress or arugula if needed)

1 romaine heart of lettuce, chopped into ½-inch (12-mm) thick strips

4 Lebanese or Persian cucumbers (or substitute 1 English cucumber), quartered and diced

1 small red onion, thinly sliced

3 small red radishes, shaved thin, preferably with mandoline

1 pint (480 g) cherry tomatoes, halved

To make the dressing, whisk together the garlic paste, lemon juice, olive oil and sumac very well in a small bowl. Check the flavor and add salt and pepper as desired. Store until ready to make the salad.

Heat the olive oil in a heavy sauce pan over medium heat. Add the freekeh and shake and stir until the grain becomes fragrant but does not burn, about 3 minutes. Add the stock with a pinch of salt and pepper. Bring to a boil. Reduce the heat to a simmer. Cover. Simmer 25 minutes or until all the liquid is absorbed. Let it cool to an ambient temperature. Freekeh can be refrigerated overnight for use the next day and will actually absorb more flavor.

Put the freekeh in a bowl and add all herbs and vegetables. Add the dressing and toss. Place on a platter and serve alone as a summer salad or with a light meal. Uneaten salad can be refrigerated and served later as a healthy, protein-rich snack.

SAMAKA HARRA WITH SUMAC SALMORIGLIO (SPICY MEDITERRANEAN FISH)

SERVES 2 TO 4

When I arrived in Boston I was shocked by not only the great variety of seafood, but by the many different ways it was prepared. Back in Lebanon, the few times we ate fish it was almost always cooked whole and either pan-fried or baked. *Samaka harra* is probably my favorite Old World whole fish recipe, with the sea bass or snapper doused in a beautiful garlic, lemon and sumac sauce.

SUMAC SALMORIGLIO SAUCE

2 cloves garlic

1 tsp crushed red pepper

1 tsp sumac

2 tbsp (30 ml) fresh lemon juice

1 tsp lemon zest

1 tbsp (4 g) parsley, finely chopped

2 tsp (12 g) salt or to taste

4 tbsp (60 ml) extra virgin olive oil

FISH

2 cloves garlic

½ jalapeño pepper, preferably red

1 tsp brined capers

Pinch of salt

2½ to 3 lb (1.1 to 1.3 kg) whole black sea bass or red snapper, scaled, gutted and gills removed

1 tbsp (15 ml) olive oil

4 circles of sliced lemon

To make the salmoriglio sauce, grind together the garlic, red pepper and sumac into a paste with a mortar and pestle. Whisk in the lemon juice, lemon zest, parsley, salt and olive oil.

When purchasing the whole sea bass or snapper, ask the fishmonger to cut into the backbone to create an extra deep cavity, or carefully do so yourself, being careful not to cut completely through the bone. Preheat the oven to 425°F (218°C). Grind the garlic, jalapeño, capers and salt into a paste. Cut two to three diagonal slashes down to the bone on each side of the fish. Rub the paste in each gash and inside the cavity, making sure to push paste into the cut bone of the cavity so that the flavor spreads into the meat. Rub the entire fish with olive oil. Place lemon slices inside the cavity. The cavity should be deep enough so that lemon slices fit completely inside. Bake on a sheet pan for about 30 minutes. Fish is done when the white meat is flaky.

Gently remove the filets from each side of the fish with two forks, being careful to leave the bones behind. Pour the salmoriglio sauce over the filets.

A BUSINESS BUILT ON HUMMUS & FALAFEL BEFORE THEY WERE COOL

Americans eat hummus today because it's healthy and versatile. We ate hummus in Beirut because it was cheap and delicious! Hummus was essential to my diet as a kid back in the old country. There was always a bowl of it sitting on the table and we might have eaten it 100 different ways.

Temptations was built on hummus and falafel. You might say those two items—two cornerstones of my culinary foundation—are where it all began for me in the business world.

Hummus, a creamy spread of chickpeas, tahini and some simple spices, is very popular these days and fairly commonplace in the American diet. Every supermarket has an entire section devoted to commercial hummus in all different flavors. But back in 1991, when I opened Temptations, hummus was something of a novelty in this country. Few Americans knew about it. I was lucky, though. I certainly caught the hummus wave at the right time.

First, there was a guy named Sami who sold Lebanese street food—hummus, falafel, wraps—out of a trailer near the hospitals in the Longwood neighborhood just down the road from Temptations. Sami has since passed away, though his namesake Sami's Wrap and Roll is still going strong. I have to give him credit. He opened Sami's before I opened Temptations and he did a lot to popularize Lebanese food, especially hummus and falafel, around Boston.

Second, Brookline is a very well-to-do community with a lot of doctors and professors who work at surrounding hospitals and universities. They're well educated and well traveled. They were more likely to know about hummus than the average American 25 years ago. Therefore, many of our customers were already familiar with hummus and those that weren't were willing to try.

And, boy, did they love it!

There's a big difference, you see, between store-bought hummus and the homemade hummus that we prepared from scratch every day for five years.

When you make something that often—it could be hummus or it could be anything—you learn all the tricks, all the ways to make it better. It becomes reflexive, part of your muscle memory.

BEIRUT TO BOSTON: A COOKBOOK

THREE SECRETS TO PERFECT HUMMUS

Follow these three tips and your hummus will come out perfect every time.

One, make your hummus with fresh, high-quality chickpeas whenever possible, as fresh chickpeas taste better and cook faster. My chickpea of choice is Palouse brand garbanzo beans (another word for chickpeas), grown in the rich farmland around Pullman, Washington.

Palouse chickpeas are Food Alliance Certified, packed fresh immediately after they're dried on the plant during the September harvest and sold within the year. Many of the commercial-grade beans on the market are several years old. Those older beans are certainly edible. In fact, you can make great, delicious hummus with any store-bought chickpea if you follow my tips and rules. But I've found those older chickpeas don't cook as quickly—which means more work for you. The typical commercial-grade chickpeas you buy in the store can take up to three hours to fatten during the boiling process; fresh chickpeas can be boiled to the perfect size and texture in just one hour. So find a good reputable local chickpea farmer.

Two, your hummus must be completely silky and creamy, with no chunks. If that means running it through the food processor for 15 minutes until it's done right, so be it. You can't hurt the hummus by overmixing it.

And, **three**, the food processor should move freely as it blends the chickpea mixture. If it slows down, slowly add some starchy water that you used to boil the chickpeas. This will loosen up the mixture so the processor can blend it perfectly. But only just enough water to get the food processor running smoothly again. You do not want the hummus too loose and watery.

CREAMY & SILKY HOMEMADE HUMMUS

This is my foundational hummus, the one upon which most of my flavored hummus is built. It is a fairly basic dish, but one that requires some time and patience to perfect because much of it is a matter of feel and instinct. I've tried to provide all my best tips in my Three Secrets to Perfect Hummus on page 103 and in the directions below. But have a little patience if your hummus doesn't come out perfect the first or second time. It will still taste delicious and you'll soon develop the "feel" for the texture that's perfect for you.

4 cups (960 ml) cold water

2 tsp (9 g) baking soda, divided

8 oz (224 g) dried high-quality chickpeas

2 cloves very fresh garlic, mashed

2 to 3 oz (58 to 87 ml) fresh lemon juice

1 cup (240 ml) high-quality tahini, shaken well before opening container

2 tsp (12 g) kosher salt

1 tsp white pepper

1 tsp cumin

1 tbsp (15 ml) extra virgin olive oil plus more to drizzle

1 tbsp (4 g) chopped parsley

Pour the water in a medium-sized bowl large enough to hold the water and chickpeas. Stir in 1 teaspoon of baking soda. Add the chickpeas. There should be enough room in the bowl to allow the peas to double in size. Soak overnight.

Rinse the chickpeas under cold water then place in a medium-sized sauce pan. Add just enough water to cover the chickpeas by 2 to 3 inches (5 to 8 cm). Add the remaining baking soda. Bring to a boil. Reduce to a simmer and cover. Fresh chickpeas, such as those recommended in my Three Secrets to Perfect Hummus (page 103) should begin to split after an hour. Commercial chickpeas can take 2 to 3 hours. When some of the chickpeas have started to split, shut off the heat. Let cool uncovered at least 2 hours. Drain the peas, reserving the starchy water. Set aside about 12 whole chickpeas to use later as garnish.

Liquify the garlic and lemon juice in a high-speed food processor for about 1 minute. Add the drained chickpeas, plus 6 ounces (175 ml) of starchy water. Blend for as long as it takes for the mixture to become completely smooth, anywhere from 4 to 10 minutes—but longer if necessary. If the mixture is so thick that the processor slows down, add some additional starchy water and the processor will regain speed. But add only enough water to get the processor running again. Add the tahini, salt, pepper and cumin and blend until completely creamy. Add the olive oil and blend that in, too. If the mixture remains chunky, it's possible that you did not cook the chickpeas long enough. The hummus will still taste fine, but will not have the perfectly creamy texture desired. Check the taste and add more salt or lemon juice if desired.

Refrigerate the hummus until ready to serve. Check its taste again when chilled and season as desired. Serve in a bowl and garnish with the reserved cooked whole chickpeas, chopped parsley and a drizzle of olive oil.

CHICKEN (BEEF OR LAMB) SHAWARMA WITH HUMMUS

SERVES 2 TO 4

Hummus alone is a delicious dip but preparing it shawarma-style makes it a meal and makes it the soul of *mazza* dining—the Lebanese version of small-plate, tapas-style plates you share with friends. Sit around the table eating chicken, beef or lamb shawarma with hummus with your family or friends. Wash it down with a few beers, a snifter of Scotch or, for true Old World flavor, some arrak, an anise-flavored spirit popular in the Middle East.

Creamy & Silky Homemade Hummus (page 105) or store-bought

Juice of ½ a lemon

1 tbsp (15 ml) olive oil

1 clove garlic, mashed

1 tbsp (18 g) kosher salt

1 tsp ground coriander

1 tsp ground cumin

1 tsp ground cardamom

1 tsp paprika

1 tbsp (4 g) finely chopped parsley, divided

8 oz (224 g) chicken breast, lamb or beef, cut into ½-inch (12-mm) strips for chicken, ¼-inch (6-mm) strips for lamb or beef

2 tbsp (17 g) pine nuts

1 tbsp (15 ml) Homemade Ghee (see page 65) or olive oil

Sprinkle of paprika and drizzle of olive oil, to garnish

First, prepare Creamy & Silky Homemade Hummus according to the directions, or substitute with your favorite store-bought hummus. Mix together the lemon juice, olive oil, garlic, salt, spices and half the parsley in a small bowl to create the marinade. Add the chicken strips. Cover and refrigerate at least 1 hour or overnight. Heat a dry sauté pan to hot. Quickly toast the pine nuts in the pan, about 2 minutes, shaking the pan the entire time so as not to burn the nuts. Remove from the heat and set the pine nuts aside. Add oil or melt ghee in the same pan and reduce the heat to medium-hot. Add the chicken strips with the entire marinade to the pan. Sauté until the chicken is browned evenly and cooked through, about 5 minutes. Remove pan from heat.

Divide the hummus among two to four small plates or shallow bowls, forming a crater in the center of the hummus. Spoon the meat evenly into the craters. Garnish each dish with the pine nuts, paprika, remaining chopped parsley and a drizzle of olive oil.

ROASTED PUMPKIN HUMMUS

SERVES 2 TO 4

I've been inspired to experiment over the years while looking for a delicious way to connect my Lebanese heritage and passion for hummus with my contemporary life in leafy, suburban New England, where roadside pumpkins are one of our signature images of autumn. This hummus made with roasted sugar pumpkins is one of the results of that effort.

We like to buy our sugar pumpkins at the Belkin Family Lookout Farm in nearby Natick, Massachusetts, which happens to be the home of Boston sports legend and fellow Lebanese-American Doug Flutie. Belkin is also one of the oldest working farms in the entire country, dating back to 1650. So there's a lot of local New England lore behind this recipe. As you might imagine, I usually make this hummus only in autumn.

ROAST PUMPKIN

1 small sugar pumpkin, no bigger than 3 lb (1.4 kg)

5 cloves garlic, unpeeled

1 to 2 tbsp (15 to 30 ml) olive oil

Salt and pepper to taste

HUMMUS

4 oz (112 g) dried chickpeas, prepared according to directions on page 105

2 oz (60 ml) fresh lemon juice

8 oz (240 ml) starchy water, reserved from preparing chickpeas

½ tbsp (9 g) kosher salt

1 tsp ground cumin

¾ cup (180 ml) tahini

1 tbsp (4 g) parsley, chopped

Sprinkle of paprika

1 tsp roasted, shelled pumpkin seeds (store-bought is fine)

Drizzle of olive oil

To roast the pumpkin, preheat the oven to 375°F (190°C). Cut the pumpkin in half. Remove the seeds, peel and cube into 2-inch (5-cm) pieces. Place on a sheet pan with the unpeeled garlic. Drizzle with olive oil. Sprinkle salt and pepper to taste. Mix around the pumpkin and garlic with oil, salt and pepper by hand to ensure the pumpkin is evenly coated. Bake for about 40 minutes, stirring the pumpkin pieces every 10 minutes or so with a spatula to ensure the pumpkin is evenly browned and caramelized. Squeeze garlic out of roasted cloves onto the pumpkin. You'll need 1 pound (454 g) of pumpkin for the hummus. Any extra pumpkin can be refrigerated to eat later. It makes a tasty snack.

Prepare the chickpeas according to the Creamy & Silky Homemade Hummus (page 105) directions, soaking overnight with baking soda, rinsing and then boiling until the chickpeas have split, while reserving the starchy water.

Add the lemon juice, about half the starchy chickpea water and roasted pumpkin and garlic to a food processor. Blend until smooth and creamy, scraping down the sides as needed. If the mixture is so thick that the processor slows down, add some additional starchy water and the processor will regain speed. Once the pumpkin is smooth, add the chickpeas, salt and cumin and blend until completely creamy. Add the tahini and stir again until creamy, adding a little bit of liquid if needed. Once the mixture is completely smooth, check the taste and add more salt or lemon juice if desired.

Refrigerate the hummus until ready to serve. Check the taste again when chilled and season as desired. Scrape into a bowl and make a well in the center of the hummus. Fill the well with a garnish of chopped parsley, paprika and roasted pumpkin seeds. Drizzle with olive oil.

AVOCADO & LIME HUMMUS

SERVES 2 TO 4

Think of this recipe as my Cinco de Mayo hummus—a sort of Mexican twist on my flagship Middle Eastern standard. You can make avocado and lime hummus anytime and serve it as you would any other hummus. It's delicious all on its own. You can also serve it as a garnish for your favorite tacos or burritos in place of guacamole.

4 oz (112 g) dried chickpeas, prepared according to directions on page 105

4 oz (120 ml) starchy water, reserved from preparing chickpeas

3 oz (87 ml) fresh lime juice

2 slightly soft avocados, peeled, pit removed and chopped or mashed

2 cloves very fresh garlic, mashed

½ tbsp (9 g) kosher salt

1 tsp freshly cracked black pepper

1 tsp ground cumin

¾ cup (180 ml) tahini

For garnish: 2 slivers fresh avocado, sprinkle of freshly cracked black pepper, pinch of sumac or paprika, drizzle of olive oil

Prepare the chickpeas according to the Creamy & Silky Homemade Hummus directions. Add the chickpeas, starchy water, lime juice, avocados, garlic, salt, pepper and cumin to the container of a high-speed food processor. Blend for as long as it takes for the mixture to become completely smooth, scraping down the sides as needed. If the mixture is so thick that the processor slows down, add some additional starchy water and the processor will regain speed. Add the tahini and blend until completely creamy again. Check the taste and add more salt or lime juice if desired.

Refrigerate the hummus until ready to serve. Check the taste again when chilled and season as desired. Transfer the hummus to a serving bowl. Form a well in the middle and fill the well with garnish: avocado slices, pepper, sumac and olive oil.

CHAPTER 5

The All-American Two-Turkey Thanksgiving

Mike's City Diner was a struggling six-month-old business when I bought it in 1996. The food it served was hit or miss and the South End neighborhood around it was still pretty rough, not the beautifully gentrified area of classic Boston brownstones and great restaurants that people see today.

It was easier in this part of the South End to find bad drugs than good food, and that's not a joke. It was a tough place to start a new business. But it was just about all I could afford; my options were limited and I needed to find a way to make money to start a family with my girlfriend and wife-to-be, Janet. Put bluntly: It was do or die time for me personally.

I had been working in the kitchen at Mike's for several months before I pulled together the money to buy out the owner. For all the challenges we faced, the diner had one great thing going for it that I was lucky to inherit: We cooked fresh turkeys every day. I knew that to make a name for ourselves, we had to do something better and different than everybody around us—a lesson which goes for any restaurant, really. And at the time nobody else in the area served fresh-cooked turkeys. Hard to believe today, when most people who eat out are obsessed with local products that are freshly cooked. But that wasn't the case in 1996, not here in this part of the South End. Most diner customers would have been content to eat over-preserved cold-cut turkey between Wonder white bread.

Turns out, though, that everybody loves fresh-cooked turkey. It's the all-American bird! So, with my future hanging in the balance, I doubled down on turkey. I dove headlong into perfecting my turkeys and everything that goes with it: the brine, the stuffing, the gravy, the mashed potatoes. We worked on those recipes day in and day out and learned a lot of tricks about turkey along the way (see page 114).

For all the effort, we got a little lucky, too. Our kitchen was so small we had nowhere to put the golden, freshly cooked turkeys when they came out of the oven. So we propped those beautiful birds right up on the steam table in the open kitchen, where people sitting at the counter or anyone who walked through the front door could see them. It was like putting raw meat in front of a pack of ravenous tigers. People saw those piping hot turkeys and they just had to order some. It was the best marketing tool imaginable. The turkeys were like a big neon sign saying "Eat at Mike's!" that everyone in the neighborhood either saw or heard about. I accidently learned a simple but valuable lesson: beautiful, freshly cooked food sells itself!

Turkey, to many Americans, is the ultimate comfort food and my South End neighbors couldn't get enough of it. So we started to serve turkey every way imaginable. Turkey hash. Turkey soup. Turkey clubs. Turkey meatloaf. Complete turkey dinners. And, of course, our signature Mike's City Diner's Famous Pilgrim Sandwich, which is basically an entire Thanksgiving dinner in a single, hand-held package. Mike's Famous Pilgrim is a very simple concept. A lot of people do their version of it, but I think we devoted more time and effort than others to making every part of the sandwich perfect. It helps, too, that we're right here in Massachusetts, not far from where the Pilgrims themselves first set foot on shore in 1620 and then celebrated the first Thanksgiving a year later.

More than 20 years later, all those turkey dishes are still on our menu every day—with various other turkey specials added from time to time. They form the foundation of Mike's City Diner. And people still go nuts for our pilgrim sandwich today. Seriously, who wouldn't want to eat a pilgrim sandwich here in Massachusetts, here in the home of the pilgrims?

We spent years building a very profitable business around those fresh-cooked turkeys, not to mention so many other diner-food classics. The neighbors loved us—largely because for some time we were the only place in the neighborhood to get fresh-cooked food. Then the politicians began to notice, especially Mayor Menino. He loved the fact that Mike's City Diner was helping to revive a once derelict neighborhood in the city he loved. He became a staunch supporter and sent plenty of business our way—including, of course, that visit from President Clinton himself.

People started to come from all over. I remember this one guy from Maine named David who would come down a couple times a year to see his daughter, a student at nearby Northeastern University, and to order a turkey dinner or pilgrim sandwich. He pulled me in close one day and whispered, "Don't tell my wife, but your turkey is better than hers!"

I don't care if you're the world's best chef or a just a guy who grills burgers in the backyard each weekend. There's nothing more satisfying than knowing that people enjoy your food. So the compliments from guests like David meant the world to me. They still do. I get up every morning hoping to see that satisfying reaction on the faces of guests when they eat my food.

The media discovered us, too. Those years of work perfecting turkey started to pay off in a wave of publicity. Guy Fieri visited before he became the international celebrity that he is today and became a very avid supporter of Mike's and, later, a friend.

"When I think about Boston, I think of Tea Party, I think of the Sox, of course, and now a place called Mike's City Diner," said Guy on the Food Network. "It's because of the way they're cranking out an American favorite: turkey!"

The Food Network later named Mike's Famous Pilgrim Sandwich one of the Top 5 Thanksgiving dishes in America. *Boston Magazine* wrote a "brief history" of the sandwich in which they described it as "a restaurant legacy." Boston restaurant critic and South End neighbor Mat Schaffer was one of my earliest supporters, always with kind things to say about us. He has one of the most sophisticated palates I know. So his support meant a lot through the years and helped Mike's City Diner build its fan base. And then one year, a few days before Thanksgiving, the *Boston Herald* put a big picture of me and one of Mike's golden turkeys on the front page under the bold-faced headline, "Bird Man!" I was thrilled by the response we were getting for our simple homespun American food.

Thanksgiving is naturally my favorite holiday because I love the food and because I truly have so much to be thankful for. We have a huge celebration at our home. My wife Janet comes from a big Irish-American family and she has 11 brothers and sisters. So we have about 50 people over for dinner. And, of course, I do all the cooking. They seem to love my gravy especially, which is made with my homemade turkey-dripping stock. We cook Thanksgiving dinner at Mike's every day of the week. But I still cherish the job of cooking dinner for our family in a big house full of guests on this great American holiday.

The irony is not lost on me: this poor kid from Lebanon somehow became known for mastering turkey, the most all-American dish on the planet. People who grew up their whole lives living here in the United States were turning to me for tips on how to cook the perfect Thanksgiving dinner. I loved every second of it and still do. I feel so thankful for all the opportunity this nation provided me and my family. So no day, no meal, is more important to me than the day and the meal we enjoy each fourth Thursday of November on Thanksgiving.

JAY'S TIPS FOR PERFECT TURKEY

Brine the bird to make it moist. Brining turkey is not exactly a secret. A lot of people know they should do it, but they just don't bother. It's too bad. It's not a lot of work, and it's really the single biggest thing you can do to make moist, tender turkey.

Dry the bird overnight for skin so crispy it snaps. Bronzed, perfectly crispy skin adds another level of flavor and texture to tasty turkey. The key is to dry your bird in the refrigerator uncovered overnight. The fridge is a perfectly dry environment that will remove excess moisture from the skin. It will crisp up better when you cook it.

Cook the bird standing up if your oven has the space. Most people cook their birds with the back down and breast up, both out of both convenience and out of tradition. Picture a Norman Rockwell family happily admiring their browned bird lying on its back at the center of the dinner table. But the best way to cook turkey is standing on its legs, with neck cavity up in the air. The fat melts in a way that makes the meat more tender. We cook thousands of turkeys at Mike's every year, and this technique is one of our signature secrets. If your oven is large enough, you should cook turkeys this way, too. We have a special metal stand with a flat base that we stick into the turkeys so that they stand up. They're often called vertical poultry roasters. You can find vertical poultry roasters online or in restaurant wholesale stores. Just make sure it's large enough to hold a turkey and not just a small chicken.

MIKE'S CITY DINER'S TURKEY BRINE

This brine is the key to delicious, moist turkey. You don't have to follow this recipe exactly. In fact, I mix it up from time to time, too. But as long as you have the right salt-to-water ratio, plus a little acid (like lemon slices) and some aromatics, the brine will work out perfectly.

32 cups (7.6 L) water
1 cup (220 g) sugar
1 cup (288 g) kosher salt
1 orange, sliced thick
1 lemon, sliced thick
4 sprigs fresh rosemary
4 sprigs fresh sage
1 bulb of garlic, halved
6 bay leaves
4 cinnamon sticks
1 (20- to 25-lb [9- to 11-kg]) turkey

Pour the water into a food-grade plastic bucket, ceramic crock or even a cooler. Mix in all the ingredients, stirring until the salt and sugar are dissolved. Place the turkey in the container. The turkey must be submerged. If not, add more water and adjust the spices accordingly. Refrigerate 48 hours, but at least 24, or let the brining container sit outdoors on a chilly seasonal night with the top covered and closed tightly. Remove the turkey from the brine. Rinse completely in the sink then pat dry. Refrigerate overnight uncovered for extra crispy skin. Cook according to directions on page 118.

THANKSGIVING TURKEY NO. 1: FOR DRIPPINGS, STOCKS AND SIDES

My two-turkey Thanksgiving begins about 5 or 6 days before the big day itself. I brine my first turkey for a day or two, and then cook it a few days before the holiday. You can brine your second bird, the one you're going to cook on Thanksgiving itself, the same day you cook the first bird.

We do not eat this first turkey, at least not right away. Instead, I use the drippings for turkey stock, which goes into my gravy, stuffing and turkey meatloaf. We use the wings, drumsticks and carcass for the stock, too. And all the dark meat goes into my turkey hash—one of the most popular dishes at Mike's City Diner! This first turkey does not have to look pretty, because nobody will see it. But they will taste it. This two-turkey technique is one of the ways I get maximum flavor out of our turkeys and all the sides and one of the reasons people think Mike's City Diner's turkeys are the best.

3 cups (710 ml) water

1 large turkey, about 20 lb (9 kg), brined 24 to 48 hours (page 115)

Preheat the oven to 350°F (176°C). Pour the water in a roasting pan. Place the turkey in the roasting pan right in the water on its back. Bake the turkey until internal temperature reaches 160°F (71 °C) when a thermometer is inserted halfway into in the thickest part of the breast, about 15 minutes per pound. However, it's more important to cook the turkey to the proper temperature, rather than for time. Remove from the oven. The turkey will continue to cook and rise to 165°F (74°C) when removed from the oven. Let the turkey cool to room temperature. Remove the breasts whole, wrap them in plastic wrap and refrigerate to make sandwiches or for additional servings of white meat on Thanksgiving.

Remove the drumsticks and wings and set them aside with the remaining carcass to use in the turkey stock. Remove the dark meat from the thigh bones and refrigerate, reserving the bones. Strain roasting pan drippings into a sauce pan through a fine-mesh strainer. Squeeze down on the remaining solids to squeeze out all the juice and flavor into the pan. Set aside the strained drippings for use in the turkey stock.

MIKE'S SIGNATURE WHOLE-TURKEY STOCK

MAKES 11 CUPS (2.6 L)

This stock is the foundation of many of the turkey dishes we cook at Mike's, including our signature stuffing and gravy, and is used in our turkey meatloaf, too. You need to cook that first bird days before Thanksgiving to have all the meat and bones to use in the stock and other sides.

24 cups (5.6 L) water

Wings, drumsticks, thigh bones, carcass and skin of 1 large cooked turkey

Drippings from cooked turkey

1 onion, quartered

1 large carrot, roughly chopped

2 stalks celery, roughly chopped

Fill a large pot with water, add the cooked wings, drumsticks, thigh bones, carcass and skin. Bring to a boil then reduce the heat and simmer about 90 minutes, or until all the meat and bones start to break down. Add more water if too much boils off. Strain very well through a cheese cloth or a fine-mesh strainer, reserving the liquid and discarding the solids. Add the stock to the drippings from the first cooked turkey, until it makes a total of 11 cups (2607 ml) of stock. For example, if you have 2 cups (480 ml) of drippings, add 9 cups (2.1 L) of stock; if you have 3 cups (710 ml) of drippings, add 8 cups (1.8 L) of stock. Mix well. Reserve 11 cups (2.6 L) of stock to use in Turkey Stuffing (page 124), Turkey Gravy (page 123) and Mike's City Diner's Turkey Meatloaf (page 121). If you have excess stock, refrigerate and use for soups or rice. Stock will freeze well, too.

THANKSGIVING TURKEY NO. 2: THE STANDING ROAST BIRD

Turkey No. 1 doesn't have to look great. After all, that first bird is being cut up to go into all my other sides. But Turkey No. 2 is the one you're going to put on the table for dinner. Mine is very simple. I don't even put salt on it. I let the flavor of the turkey speak for itself. But I do stand the bird up on a poultry roaster to cook it, which is our signature method to achieve maximum tenderness. This is the exact same way we cook the delicious turkeys that made Mike's City Diner synonymous with Thanksgiving dinner.

3 cups (710 ml) water

1 large turkey, about 20 lb (9 kg), brined 24 to 48 hours (page 115)

1 vertical poultry roaster or other oven-safe stand

Brine the turkey one to two days before Thanksgiving (see page 115 for brine recipe). Refrigerate the turkey uncovered overnight to dry out the skin, which will help make it extra crispy when cooked. Preheat the oven to 350°F (176°C). Pour water in a roasting pan. Insert a poultry roaster into the turkey cavity so that the bird appears to stand up on its legs. Cooking the turkey standing up helps create a moister, tastier bird and is one of our signature turkey secrets at Mike's City Diner. Bake the turkey until the internal temperature reaches 160°F (71°C) when a thermometer is inserted halfway into in the thickest part of the breast, about 15 minutes per pound. However, it's more important to cook the turkey to the proper temperature, rather than for time. Remove from the oven. The turkey will continue to cook and rise to 165°F (73°C) when removed from the oven. Let the turkey rest 30 minutes. Carve and serve.

MIKE'S CITY DINER'S TURKEY MEATLOAF

SERVES 8 TO 10

Dash of olive oil

2 medium onions, finely chopped

3 cloves garlic, crushed

3 tbsp (54 g) kosher salt

2 tsp (4 g) black pepper

¼ cup (60 ml) Worcestershire sauce

1 cup (240 ml) Mike's Signature Whole-Turkey Stock (see page 117), or substitute with favorite poultry stock

1 tbsp (16 g) tomato paste

5 lb (2.2 kg) fresh ground turkey

2 cups (216 g) bread crumbs

3 eggs

1 cup (240 ml) ketchup

Preheat the oven to 375°F (190°C). Heat the oil in a sauté pan with onions, garlic, salt and pepper until the onion is translucent. Add the Worcestershire sauce, stock and tomato paste and mix well. Let cool to room temperature. Combine the ground turkey, breadcrumbs, eggs and onion mixture in a large bowl. Mix well and shape into a rectangular loaf in a bread pan or simply shape it on an ungreased sheet pan. Spread the ketchup on the top. Bake for 1 hour or until the internal temperature reaches 160°F (71°C). Wait about 10 minutes then slice.

MASON JAR CRANBERRY SAUCE

These mason jars of sauce, decorated with ribbon or other holiday décor, look great on the dinner table and also make a colorful and festive Thanksgiving or Christmas party gift.

1½ lb (672 g) cranberries

2 cups (400 g) sugar

2 cups (240 ml) water

½ orange, with peel, cut into small cubes

2 tbsp (14 g) pecans or walnuts, crushed (optional)

Remove a handful of cranberries and set aside. Combine the sugar and water in a large pot with the cranberries and orange pieces. Bring to a boil, then reduce to a simmer for about 10 minutes, stirring occasionally. Add the reserved cranberries and optional nuts near the end of the simmer. Cover and remove from heat. Pour the hot sauce into very clean mason jars. Cool to room temperature. Refrigerate until ready to serve.

TURKEY GRAVY

The gravy we serve at Mike's City Diner is very delicious and surprisingly simple. Guests and even chefs are surprised to find that we don't even put any poultry herbs in it, like you find in most gravies. The reason is very simple: We've got tons of great turkey flavor right from that natural, homemade stock.

5 cups (1185 ml) Mike's Signature Whole-Turkey Stock (see page 117)

4 tbsp (56 g) unsalted butter

½ cup (62 g) all-purpose flour

Kosher salt and pepper to taste

Warm the stock in a medium-sized sauce pan. Melt the butter in a separate 2-quart (1.8-L) sauce pan over medium-low heat. Whisk the flour into the butter briskly for 1 to 2 minutes, until the flour is cooked through. Slowly pour half the warm stock into the roux and whisk it well. When the mixture thickens, whisk in the remaining stock. Bring to a boil for about 1 to 2 minutes. To thicken, reduce the heat and simmer to desired texture. Salt and pepper as desired.

TURKEY STUFFING

SERVES 8 TO 12

This is my favorite stuffing, the same we serve at Mike's City Diner. There are no gimmicks or bells and whistles, like cornbread or chestnuts. Just plenty of homemade turkey stock and good, old-fashioned hearty all-American flavor.

2 large loaves of French or Italian bread, a total of 2 lb (908 g)

2 tbsp (28 g) unsalted butter

1 cup (160 g) diced yellow onion

½ cup (55 g) shredded carrot

½ cup (50 g) diced celery

5 cups (1.1 L) Mike's Signature Whole-Turkey Stock (see page 117)

½ tsp dried thyme

½ tsp poultry seasoning

Break up the bread by hand and let sit overnight in large bowl to turn dry and slightly stale.

The next day, preheat the oven to 350°F (176°C). Melt the butter over medium heat, and sauté the onion, carrots and celery (a *mirepoix*) until the onion is translucent and the carrots and celery are softened. Pour the butter and the mirepoix over the bread. Pour warm stock over the entire mixture. Add the thyme and poultry seasoning. Mix well with a wooden spoon. The mixture should be very moist. Pour into a 9 × 13-inch (23 × 33-cm) casserole or baking dish. Bake for 30 minutes. The stuffing should have a beautiful crust on top but will be moist inside.

Note: Prepare the stuffing a day ahead of time and pour into a baking dish, then refrigerate overnight and bake after the turkey comes out of the oven and is cooling.

TURKEY HASH

SERVES 6 TO 8

Turkey hash is one of our signature specialties at Mike's City Diner and the perfect way to get rid of all that leftover dark meat from the legs and thighs of your Thanksgiving bird. It's become one of our most beloved items over the years.

2 lb (908) boiled Yukon gold potatoes, divided

4 tbsp (56 g) unsalted butter, plus more for frying

5 oz (140 g) raw bacon, cut into ¼-inch (6.3-mm) strips

1 large yellow onion, diced

½ cup (75 g) finely diced green bell pepper

1 tbsp (18 g) salt or to taste

1 tsp black pepper

½ tsp cayenne

1 lb (454 g) dark turkey meat, roughly chopped

¼ cup (15 g) finely chopped fresh parsley

1 tbsp (4 g) roughly chopped fresh sage

½ cup chicken stock

Mash half the boiled potatoes with a fork; roughly and unevenly chop the remaining potatoes. Set the potatoes aside.

Melt the butter over medium heat in a medium-sized sauce pot. Sauté the bacon in the melted butter. Let them sizzle together about 3 minutes to start rendering. Add the onion, bell pepper, salt, pepper and cayenne. Sauté about 8 minutes, until the onions start browning and the pepper softens. Stir occasionally.

Add the turkey meat, parsley and sage. Mix well and let cook about 2 to 3 minutes. Add the stock to deglaze the pan. Scrape the pan well with a wooden spoon. Add the potatoes and mix well. It should not be a loose mixture. It should be firm and bound together well.

Let the hash cool to room temperature then refrigerate overnight for the best flavor, though the hash can be cooked immediately.

Preheat the oven to 400°F (204°C).

Form the hash into patties about 1 cup (240 ml) in size. Melt a dollop of butter in a nonstick pan over medium-high heat. Flatten the hash in the pan under a bacon press. Sear for about 5 minutes until the bottom forms a nice crisp, caramelized edge. Flip and sear the other side in same way. Or, if desired, flatten the entire mixture in an oven-safe nonstick pan and bake for about 25 minutes. Serve with your favorite eggs or as a side dish with brunch.

MIKE'S CITY DINER'S FAMOUS PILGRIM SANDWICH

This is the sandwich that put Mike's City Diner on the map, beloved by a generation of Bostonians and proclaimed by the Food Network as one of the five best Thanksgiving meals in America. It's beautiful, messy, savory and delicious! A true taste of autumn in New England that we serve every day of the year.

1 braided roll or other favorite sandwich roll

2 to 3 tbsp (30 to 45 ml) freshly made Mason Jar Cranberry Sauce (page 122)

½ to 1 cup (120 to 240 ml) Turkey Stuffing (page 124)

8 to 10 oz (224 to 280 g) freshly sliced Thanksgiving Turkey No. 1 white meat (page 116)

½ cup (120 ml) warm Turkey Gravy (page 123)

Spread the cranberry sauce on the bottom roll. Then layer the stuffing and turkey on top. Pour gravy all over the sandwich. Top the sandwich with the other half of the roll. Eat with a knife and fork.

CHAPTER 6

Blessed in Boston

Images of Beirut lingered in my mind during my teenage and young adult years—my school playground next to the church, which I could see from our apartment window, the little bodega on the bottom floor of our building where I'd buy candy and gum and the streets and alleys where we'd play ball with the other kids or collect bullet casings after the fighting. These memories called to me during all my years in Boston.

Beirut was, in my heart, my hometown. It held great memories for me, despite the death and violence. Remember, the war didn't scare us as kids. We didn't know any different. So I really didn't harbor too many bad memories, even though we had seen some very bad things.

All I remembered is that Beirut was (and is) a beautiful city. People called it the Paris of the East, both for its architectural beauty and for its French influence. In addition to great memories, I also harbored this innate love for my ancestral homeland. I was proud to be Lebanese. I'm still proud to be Lebanese. I was also proud to be from Beirut. I'm still proud to be from Beirut, this beautiful, historic city on the Mediterranean.

So, just before purchasing Mike's City Diner in 1996, I returned to Beirut for the first time since I was a small boy in the 1970s.

Beirut was my hometown. I wanted to see the church and my school, the streets and alleys and my relatives, too. And, of course, I had to see the village in Maasser El Chouf where we lived with my grandmother one winter to escape war, my father's hometown of Machghara, where we often spent our summers and the village of Zahle, where my cousins owned a beautiful flower farm and where we'd go for family picnics. I also wanted to visit the marina in Jounieh right on the Mediterranean where my brothers and I would fish from the dock, using only a bamboo stick with string and a hook and bread for bait.

My cousin Elias picked me up at the airport that day in 1995, and immediately brought me back first to the old neighborhood, Ain el-Remmaneh, back into "the Eye of the Pomegranate." I assumed I would step off the plane, see my relatives and the old streets and feel it was just like old times. But it didn't feel like old times. In fact, much to my surprise, I felt like a stranger in a strange land.

The Lebanese, my people, are the nicest people in the world, with great food and warm hospitality. But soon after arriving, it hit me like a bolt of lightning why my parents had left behind all they knew: to give us a better life. Lebanon, for all its great culture, beauty and history, was an old, tired country in a dangerous part of the world. It struck me as very needy and in some ways very sad. The people there simply do not have the opportunities we have here in America. It dawned on me that I was no longer Lebanese. I was an American now. I had adopted the

American culture, mannerism and attitudes, and maybe even grown a little spoiled by the things we take for granted here, like regular trash collection, a steady stream of running water in your bathroom or electricity when you need it in the middle of the night. Much to my surprise, I felt like a foreigner in the land of my birth.

My mind started racing: What would have happened to us if we had stayed here in Beirut? What would have happened if we had never landed in Boston, if we had never arrived in this amazing country called America? All these thoughts flooded over me soon after arriving in Beirut.

I knew life would have been so much different if we had stayed in Beirut, assuming we even survived the war. I swelled with gratitude for my adopted homeland, for the life it afforded me, for the opportunities the United States gives so many people, opportunities that, unfortunately, don't exist in many other parts of the world. Opportunities that don't exist in places like Beirut, no matter how much I love my birthplace.

I was filled with pride in America and thought to myself right there and then, "I'd fight and die for the United States, the greatest place on Earth."

That feisty patriotism still swelled inside my heart nearly 20 years later, on Monday, April 15, 2013. It was Patriots Day in Massachusetts, the day Boston hosts its world-famous marathon and the day we celebrate the Minutemen who stood up to the British in nearby Lexington and Concord, launching the American Revolution.

That beautiful April morning was also the day a pair of terrorists ignited two deadly bombs at the finish line of the Boston Marathon on Boylston Street, just five blocks from Mike's City Diner. Three beautiful young people were killed and hundreds more maimed. Right here in my neighborhood! I was pissed off, just like millions of Bostonians. My anger was made stronger by the sad fact that the religion-fueled terror I lived through as a child in the Middle East had now come to the historic old streets of my beloved Boston, the very city where America began, where the American Dream began. It was the city that embraced me and my family. The city that made me who I am today. And now this beautiful city I loved looked like a war zone.

Red Sox star David Ortiz summed up the attitude Bostonians felt days later when, standing in the middle of the field at Fenway Park, he blurted out in front of 35,000 people and into millions of homes, "This is our fucking city!"

It was crude. But he got the point across. You mess with one Bostonian, you mess with all of us. His words have since become a rallying cry for the millions of us who love Boston. Oh, you don't like us? Too bad. "This is our fucking city!" Little did I know at the time that, a couple years later, Ortiz and I would become two of the partners behind Yvonne's, the beautiful supper club in downtown Boston's culinary landmark Locke-Ober building.

From the moment of the first explosion, Bostonians rallied to help each other—you can see it in so many of those images caught on film and broadcast around the world. Being chefs, we tried to help the only way we know how. By cooking and feeding people. It may not be much, but it's what we do.

My friend Ken Oringer might be the most talented chef I know. You name an ingredient or a type of cuisine, and he knows all about it. He's won all kinds of awards and owns restaurants here in Boston and around the world, including Toro, the beautiful tapas restaurant right next door to Mike's City Diner. Within days of the bombing, he teamed with Boston celebrity chef Ming Tsai to plan an incredible event called Boston Bites Back. About 100 local chefs prepared their favorite dishes and served them at Fenway Park, just one month after the marathon bombing. I prepared my falafel with an avocado tahini and stuffed it in tiny pita pockets shaped with a cookie cutter. All the dishes were delicious and the event was a huge success. Thanks to incredible support from so many people, we raised $1 million in one night for The One Fund, which helped many victims of the bombing, and helped reinforce the sense of community that makes Boston a big city that feels like a small town.

We've since developed something of a charity circuit, with pop-up dinners here at Mike's City Diner featuring our chef friends like Ken, Ming, Jamie Bissonnette and so many others. A year after the Marathon bombing, and just a few blocks away, two Boston firefighters were tragically killed battling a blaze in a brownstone in the Back Bay neighborhood. Ed Walsh and Michael Kennedy worked at the Engine 33 firehouse, right up the street from Mike's City Diner. They were my neighbors and I've met them and so many neighborhood firefighters. I don't remember specifically, but they may have eaten here at Mike's, too, like so many cops and firefighters do. So I pulled together a dinner here at Mike's called United for Boston's Own, again with the top chefs of Boston. I prepared grilled lamb with harissa sauce, one of my favorites. In the space of one night here in this tiny little 50-seat diner, we raised $50,000 for the families of the firefighters.

In 2015, Philadelphia chef Ed Kulp was paralyzed in an Amtrak train accident. Ken and I organized another pop-up fundraiser here at Mike's. Few of us here in Boston knew Ed. Still, he was a chef, a member of our extended community. So, once again, we all jammed into the kitchen at Mike's to whip up our favorite dishes for very generous patrons who spent $500 per person just to eat our food for charity. And before that, in 2012, we cooked to raise money for the Red Cross to help victims of Hurricane Sandy. Regardless of the cause, we all have a great time cooking together.

Sometimes we get together here at Mike's to cook just for fun, too. When chef Stephanie Izard of the Girl & the Goat restaurant in Chicago came to Boston to promote her book, *Girl in the Kitchen*, it seemed like a perfectly good reason for another pop-up at Mike's. I made one of my all-time favorite dishes that night, Turkish-Style Stuffed Mussels (page 135), a savory mixture of rice and spices carefully packed between the shells, and then steamed until cooked through. The mussels are delicious and beautiful, almost a conversation piece.

Our little contributions may not have meant much in the big scheme of things, but a lot of little acts by a lot of different people add up and, I believe, help make a better community. It's the least we can do as chefs to pay back society for all the blessings we enjoy living, working and cooking in this wonderful diverse country.

It's the same feeling I had that day I returned to Beirut for the first time. I can't tell you exactly when, but I know by the time I got back to America I thanked my lucky stars that the Hajj family arrived in Boston, stayed in Boston and were embraced by Boston.

TURKISH-STYLE STUFFED MUSSELS

This recipe is a little labor intensive. You have to carefully slice open each mussel, and then pack each with the rice stuffing. But I find the effort both therapeutic and rewarding. And if you really want to impress people with a beautiful and creative party appetizer with some global flavor, you'd be hard pressed to do better than these delicious mussels.

2 tbsp (30 ml) olive oil

1 medium yellow onion, diced fine

¼ cup (37 g) finely diced red pepper

2 cloves garlic, mashed

½ cup (100 g) short-grain white rice

1½ tbsp (24 g) tomato paste

2 tbsp (8 g) chopped fresh parsley

2 tbsp (32 g) raisins, roughly chopped

½ tsp cinnamon

½ tsp allspice

½ tsp paprika

¼ tsp cayenne pepper

Pinch of saffron

2 tsp (12 g) salt or to taste

1 cup (240 ml) chicken stock

1 to 1¼ lb (454 to 680 g) medium to large mussels, 20 to 30 mussels

Heat the oil in a medium-sized sauce pan over medium heat. Stir in the onion, red pepper, garlic and rice. Stir to coat the rice with oil, about 3 minutes. Stir in the tomato paste, parsley, raisins, all the spices and salt. Mix well, then add the stock. Cover and simmer about 8 to 10 minutes or until all moisture evaporates. Remove from the heat and let cool to room temperature. Clean the mussel shells and discard beards, if any. Rinse the shells in cold water. Shuck the mussels by inserting a slim clam knife by the back hinge, then slide the knife through the concave side of the mussel to break the muscle holding the shells together near the tip. Flip each shell open. There should be meat on each side. Fill each shell with just enough mixture, so that the shells can be closed back together. Stack stuffed shells in top of double steamer in a flat, organized way. Cook 25 to 30 minutes over slow steam. Line the stuffed shells on a serving tray or cutting board, with the top shell removed to expose stuffing and mussel meat.

MING TSAI'S WHIPPED EDAMAME HUMMUS WITH SPICED PITA CHIPS

SERVES 4

Ming Tsai is one of America's most successful chefs and has been an inspiration on a number of levels, namely with his signature East Meets West fusion of Asian and American cooking. This recipe is a Japanese-influenced version of my favorite thing to make, homemade hummus, using edamame instead of chickpeas.

EDAMAME HUMMUS

1 (10-oz [280-g]) bag of frozen edamame

2 tbsp (30 ml) Greek yogurt

¼ cup (35 g) roasted garlic

2 tbsp (12 g) ground cumin

2 tbsp (12 g) ground coriander

Juice of 1 lemon

1 tsp sesame oil

Olive oil

Togarashi to taste (Japanese chili powder)

Salt and pepper to taste

SPICED PITA CHIPS:

1 package whole wheat pita bread

1 tbsp (6 g) chili powder

1 tbsp (6 g) onion powder

1 tbsp (6 g) garlic powder

½ tbsp salt

½ tbsp black pepper

Olive oil

For the edamame hummus, cook the edamame in a pot of boiling salted water until they are soft, about 20 minutes. Drain completely. Blend edamame in a food processor with the Greek yogurt. Add roasted garlic, cumin, coriander, lemon juice and sesame oil. Slowly add the olive oil as necessary to mix until smooth. Add togarashi, salt and pepper to taste. Stir to combine. Refrigerate until ready to serve.

Preheat the oven to 350°F (176°C). Halve each piece of pita bread vertically and cut into 2½-inch (6-cm) wedges. Mix all the dry ingredients together in a bowl. Brush both sides of the pita bread lightly with olive oil. Sprinkle both sides of the pita bread lightly with the spice mixture and place on a baking sheet and bake until golden brown and crisp, turning once, 5 to 7 minutes. Let pitas cool slightly and serve with the edamame hummus.

MY BEST BUDDY'S SHAKSHUKA

Guy's Cooking with Best Buddies is a great event here in Boston each summer, featuring Food Network chef and friend Guy Fieri, New England Patriots quarterback Tom Brady and about two dozen Boston chefs.

Tom stars in a charity touch football game, while we all cook some of our signature dishes. It's a great event with delicious food and wine. Most importantly, we raise a lot of money for Best Buddies International, which helps people around the world cope with intellectual and developmental disabilities.

Guy is a great chef and a great friend. He has welcomed me into his home and onto his Food Network shows many times over the years. And I've been lucky enough to be a part of Best Buddies since the very beginning, back when there were only about five chefs involved. My Best Buddy is Sarah Markowitz. She's an inspiring young lady and she helps our team prepare our food for the event each year. I've grown close with the Markowitz family and in my world "close" means that we get together to cook for each other and, of course, to eat!

One time Sarah's dad Mike Markowitz cooked shakshuka for us. It's a traditional Israeli dish of eggs poached in a tomato-and-spice stew. It's rich, luxurious and delicious! It also reminded me of a dish my mom used to make for us back in Beirut. But our version was not quite as luxurious.

Food could be scarce back then and we couldn't afford to let any go to waste. So if we had some tomatoes that started to go bad, my mom would cook them down into a stew with eggs—a sort of poor man's shakshuka. My mother never cooked that stew again once we arrived in the United States. So when I ate it that time with the Markowitz family, it instantly reminded me of my childhood in Beirut. That breakfast at the Markowitz home that morning made me realize how much I had missed that childhood memory. I've since made shakshuka a part of my culinary repertoire. This recipe is a tribute to my Best Buddy Sarah, her great family and a fond childhood memory.

¼ cup (60 ml) olive oil

1 large yellow onion, diced

1 tsp kosher salt, or to taste

½ tsp black pepper, or to taste

1 red pepper, chopped

5 cloves garlic, roughly chopped

2 tbsp (32 g) tomato paste

1 tsp ground cumin

1 tsp Aleppo pepper

1 tsp paprika

¼ tsp crushed red pepper

1 (28-oz [784-g]) can high-quality whole peeled tomatoes with liquid

¼ cup plus 1 tbsp (46 g) crumbled feta cheese, divided

6 eggs

2 tbsp (2 g) roughly chopped fresh cilantro

(continued)

MY BEST BUDDY'S SHAKSHUKA (CONT.)

Preheat the oven to 400°F (204°C). Heat the oil in a 10-inch (25-cm) heavy skillet. Add the onion, salt and black pepper and sauté 3 to 4 minutes, stirring occasionally. Reduce the heat to medium-low. Add the red pepper and sauté 15 minutes, stirring occasionally, until the onion and pepper are very soft. Add the garlic and sauté until the garlic turns fragrant, about 2 minutes. Add the tomato paste, cumin, Aleppo pepper, paprika and crushed red pepper and mix well. Add the canned tomatoes with juice and increase the heat to medium-high. Stir well while gently breaking up the whole tomatoes with wooden spoon. Reduce until the tomato thickens, about 10 to 15 minutes. Turn off the heat.

Stir in ¼ cup (37 g) crumbled feta cheese. Gently crack the eggs on top of the mixture, evenly spaced. Place the entire skillet in a preheated oven for 5 minutes for soft eggs or until eggs are cooked through as desired. Garnish with the remaining tablespoon (9 g) of feta cheese and cilantro. Scoop onto a dinner plate or bowl and serve with your favorite crusty bread.

JAMIE BISSONNETTE'S SHAWARMA LAMB PAELLA

SERVES 8

Jay Hajj is one of the best chefs I have ever met. He's obsessed. He's a natural. He's fanatical. When we were in Dubai, on our way to Bangkok to open my restaurant Toro there, we went to the spice souk, or open-air market. On the way there we grabbed a quick shawarma. We got it "Mexican style," meaning spicy. It was a crazy bite of food. We savored it and analyzed it. I'll never forget it.

The following week, Jay and I bounced around Bangkok, eating and exploring as much as possible. We were talking about this book, and he asked if I would contribute a recipe. I knew we had to take the flavors we had in Dubai and make it into a paella. I kept thinking about all the times he cooked meze for us at Toro in Boston and all the delicious ingredients he has introduced us to. So this recipe is inspired by Jay, by our travels and by our friendship.
—Jamie Bissonnette

SHAWARMA LAMB

10 cloves

6 green cardamom pods

2 star anise

1 cinnamon stick

1 tbsp (6 g) whole cumin

1 tbsp (6 g) whole fennel seeds

2 tsp (6 g) black peppercorns

2 tsp (7 g) fenugreek seeds

1 tbsp (7 g) Pimenton de la Vera (or other smoked paprika)

1 tsp ground turmeric

1 cup (240 ml) sunflower oil (or canola oil)

Juice of 1 lemon

1 tbsp (6 g) lemon zest, minced

6 garlic cloves, minced

4 oz (112 g) ginger root, peeled and minced

Kosher salt to taste

3 lb (1362 g) boneless lamb shoulder

1 cup (240 ml) white wine or water

To make the shawarma, preheat the oven to 350°F (176°C). Toast the cloves, cardamom, star anise, cinnamon, cumin, fennel, peppercorns and fenugreek in a heavy-bottom pan. Add the toasted spices to a spice grinder with the paprika and turmeric. Pulse into a powder as fine as possible, but some texture is OK. In a large bowl, add the spices to the oil, lemon juice, lemon zest, garlic, ginger and salt. Mix to combine.

Make several deep slices into the lamb shoulder, but do not cut all the way through. Rub the mixture all over the meat, getting it everywhere inside and out. Truss the meat with twine to hold it together. Cook the lamb on a roasting tray uncovered until internal temperature reaches 155°F (68°C), 60 to 90 minutes. Baste the lamb with wine or water occasionally. If the meat appears to get too dark and looks like it will burn, cover with foil. Remove from the oven and let the meat rest at least 30 minutes before slicing. You can also let the meat cool to room temperature then refrigerate overnight. The meat is easier to slice when cold. Save all the juices as you thinly slice the meat and refrigerate any unused meat in the juices. You only need 1 pound (454 g) for the paella so you can save the rest for later.

(continued)

SALAD

2 cups (72 g) sliced little gem lettuce

1 cup (52 g) cucumbers (Persian are the best), diced or sliced and coiled for effect

1 cup (180 g) chopped very ripe heirloom tomatoes (use only very ripe tomatoes, otherwise skip)

1 cup (240 ml) Lebanese-Style Pickled Turnips (see page 144), thinly sliced

Kosher salt and pepper to taste

Dash of sumac

PAELLA

3 tbsp plus ¼ cup (105 ml) extra virgin olive oil, divided

4 oz (112 g) favorite lamb sausage (optional)

2 garlic cloves, crushed and minced

1 cup (160 g) peeled and diced Spanish onion

¼ cup (25 g) sliced scallion bottoms

1 tsp kosher salt

1 tsp fresh cracked black pepper

½ cup (75 g) sunchokes, cut into bite sized pieces

¼ cup (66 g) tomato paste

1 tbsp (6 g) Baharat (Middle Eastern spice mix)

½ cup (75 g) seeded and diced red bell pepper,

1 cup (200 g) Calasparra or Bomba rice

10 threads of saffron

4½ cups (1066 ml) chicken stock

1 lb (454 g) shawarma lamb (page 141), sliced thin

¼ cup (25 g) sliced scallion tops

2 tbsp (2 g) chopped mint

1 cup (240 ml) Tahini Sauce (page 93)

Moroccan-Style Harissa Sauce (page 160), to taste

JAMIE BISSONNETTE'S SHAWARMA LAMB PAELLA (CONT.)

For the salad, mix the little gem, cucumbers, tomatoes and pickled turnips in a bowl. Season with salt, pepper and sumac. Scatter over the paella or serve on the side as a salad.

To make the paella, use a paella pan or shallow, heavy-bottom Dutch oven, add 3 tablespoons (45 ml) olive oil, lamb sausage, garlic, onion, scallion bottoms, salt and pepper and sauté 4 to 5 minutes over medium-high heat. Add the sunchokes, tomato paste, Baharat and bell pepper and cook 2 minutes. Add the rice and saffron. Stir to evenly coat the rice and toast it 4 to 5 minutes. Evenly distribute and flatten out rice in the pan. Add the stock and increase the heat to high. Season with more salt. Bring to a boil, then reduce to a simmer and cook about 10 minutes, rotating the paella pan every 2 minutes.

Lay the sliced lamb all over the top of the paella. Remember to keep the pan at a good low simmer, as you want to cook the rice without burning, but you do not want to stir it. Cook about 5 to 8 more minutes or until the rice is plump and cooked through. Taste, and adjust with salt and pepper. Keep on high heat and continue to rotate the pan every 2 minutes to create an even, crispy bottom, called *socorrat*. Add stock or water if you need more moisture for the rice to cook through. Garnish with the remaining ¼ cup (60 ml) olive oil, scallion tops and mint. Drizzle the tahini and harissa sauces over the top or serve on the side.

LEBANESE-STYLE PICKLED TURNIPS

Pickled turnips are a very common side or condiment in the Lebanese kitchen. I serve them with almost everything. You can eat pickled turnips with Chicken Liver Pâté (see page 42), with Homestyle Labneh (see page 53), with Manakish (see page 58), on a meze plate or even on its own. Basically, make these pickled turnips and serve them with anything that needs a little added pizzazz of flavor and color.

5 small to medium turnips

1 small to medium beet

4 cloves garlic

2½ cups (600 ml) water

1½ cups (360 ml) distilled white vinegar

3 tbsp (42 g) kosher salt or sea salt

Wash and peel the turnips and the beet. Slice into matchsticks, about ¼-inch to ½-inch (6- to 8-mm) wide, or roughly the size of a French fry. Add garlic to two clean and sterilized quart (liter) pickling jars. Fill each jar with turnip and beet matchsticks. The beets help add a nice reddish color to the turnip and should be sprinkled across the bottom, middle and top of each jar.

Combine the water, vinegar and salt in a sauce pan. Bring to a boil. Quickly remove from the heat and pour hot water into each jar, leaving 1 inch (2.5 cm) of space at the top, but making sure all the turnip is covered by liquid. Close jars with sterilized caps and turn them upside down on a kitchen towel and let sit this way about 2 hours to help seal tightly. Pickled turnips should last at least 6 months in a cupboard. Refrigerate after opening.

BATINJAN MAKDOUS (PICKLED STUFFED BABY EGGPLANT)

Batinjan makdous is of my favorite memories of childhood in Lebanon. My mom always had a few jars of these delicious stuffed eggplants sitting around the house. She'd also make sandwiches with them that we'd take to school. Our school was so rudimentary that we didn't have a cafeteria. So I can still smell that intense aroma of garlic and olive oil all over the classroom!

I still make jars of batinjan makdous at my house today and keep them in my pickling cabinet. These stuffed egg-plants make great table-top tapas and they're a delicious side, making most any dish more flavorful. I also serve them as passed appetizers at parties and fundraisers and as part of meze or charcuterie boards with hummus, bread, labneh or mozzarella cheese and favorite meats.

1 cup (117 g) walnuts, chopped

2 heads peeled garlic cloves

4 tsp (24 g) kosher salt

2 tsp (3 g) finely chopped red bell pepper or 1 jalapeño

18 to 20 baby eggplants

High-quality extra-virgin olive oil

Pulse the walnuts in a food processor 6 or 7 times until crushed well. Set aside in a small bowl. Place the garlic cloves in a food processor and mix until very finely ground. Add to the walnuts. Stir in the kosher salt and red bell or jalapeño pepper and mix well. Wash the eggplants and peel off the loose leaves of the stem by hand. Cut off the remaining stem, through the green stem bottom, just above the dark skin of the eggplant. This small remaining bit of stem will help the eggplants hold their shape after cooking and canning.

Put the eggplants in large pot with enough water to cover them. Place a plate on top of the eggplants to hold them down and help them cook evenly. Bring to a boil. Then shut off the heat, cover the pot and let the eggplants steep in hot water for 15 minutes. They should be soft but not very tender. Place the eggplants in a colander and again top with weight—three plates are ideal—to help press out excess liquid. Drain for 45 minutes.

Cut a slit in one side of each eggplant, being careful not to rip open the ends. Stuff each eggplant with about 1 tablespoon (15 g) of mixture. Arrange the eggplants in two 32-ounce (945-ml) pickling jars, first sterilized according to directions on the package. Eggplants should be snug but not packed tight, two eggplants per layer, arranged so that the skinny end of one layer sits on top of the fat end of another layer. Fill each jar with olive oil, leaving 1 inch (2.5 cm) of space on the top of the jar. Close the jar tightly with a sterilized cap. Let sit at least 10 days before serving.

SMOKY VENISON BREAKFAST SAUSAGE

Joshua Smith of Moody's Delicatessen & Provisions in Waltham, just west of Boston, is one of the smartest chefs in town and his charcuterie is second to none. In fact, he's my go-to guy for any advice on making charcuterie.

I met Joshua a couple years ago while helping my friend Kerry J. Byrne, the Boston food writer and the co-author of this book, make his family-favorite smoky venison breakfast sausage. Kerry prepares the sausage for a big breakfast fundraiser he hosts each Thanksgiving called the Pigskin Gala. The event features these homemade sausage and bacon and even the turkey hash we serve at Mike's City Diner.

We make so much sausage for the Pigskin Gala that it outgrew our ability to do it in the home kitchen. So Josh was kind enough one year to let us use the equipment at his incredible smokehouse, New England Charcuterie. We were really impressed by Josh's operation, which he designed himself and which turns out some of the most delicious and savory charcuterie you'll ever taste.

Josh and I have since become friends, while Kerry now asks Josh each year to make the smoky venison sausage for his big party. Always best to leave it to the experts! But you can try your hand at a smaller version of the same recipe pretty easily at home with a kitchen meat grinder, sausage stuffer and backyard smoker. These sausages are delicious and full of great autumn-in-New-England aroma and flavor.

8 lb (3.6 kg) chilled venison, preferably chunks of stew meat

2 lb (908 g) beef fat or suet

5 tbsp (90 g) salt

4 tsp (5 g) sage

4 tsp (9 g) ground nutmeg

2 tsp (2 g) ground white pepper

1½ tsp (2 g) ground ginger

2 tbsp (12 g) powdered dextrose

2 tsp (10 g) Insta Cure No. 1

2 cups (480 ml) water, divided

Lemon juice or Mason Jar Cranberry Sauce (page 122), to serve

Grind the meat chunks and fat in a sausage grinder and into a large stainless steel or disposable aluminum or steel pan. Try to evenly disperse the fat throughout the grinding process. Add the salt, sage, nutmeg, white pepper, ginger, powdered dextrose and Insta Cure and about half the water. Mix well with clean, bare hands.

Run half the meat through the grinder once more. If the meat seems a little tough to get through the grinder (the dextrose will make it thick) add the rest of the water at this point. When half of the meat has gone through the grinder a second time, add any remaining water and again mix well with bare hands, making sure the spices and the once-ground meat are evenly dispersed. Using a sausage stuffer, stuff the meat into cleaned and soaked hog casings. Add more water to the meat mixture as needed, as the powdered dextrose is a binder that will stiffen the meat.

After stuffing, hang all the sausage in a cool, dry place for at least 2 hours. Then place all the sausage in a 110°F (43°C) smoker, gradually raising the smoker temperature to 160°F (71°C) to achieve an internal temperature of 152°F (67°C) in the sausage, about 4 to 6 hours. The sausage should sweat a bit and develop a dark, smoky brown autumn color. Grill or pan-fry the sausage in heavy skillet until heated through. Serve with a splash of lemon or cranberry sauce. Unused sausage can be wrapped in freezer paper, frozen and defrosted when ready to serve.

YVONNE'S OYSTERS SAVANNAH

When my real estate partners and I bought the landmark Locke-Ober building in Boston's Downtown Crossing back in 2012, we knew we wanted to fill the space with a beautiful contemporary restaurant. But we wanted a restaurant that still honored the tradition of Locke-Ober, Boston's most famous and most luxurious dining destination for more than a century.

Yvonne's fit the bill on both counts. It's a modern supper club with a library lounge, gorgeous bar, sumptuous décor, great cocktails and incredible food from culinary director Tom Berry, executive chef Juan Pedrosa and their team. And, yes, they pay tribute to the legacy of Locke-Ober with both the design of the restaurant and with menu items such as oysters Savannah, a re-interpretation of Locke-Ober's original signature dish, Locke-Ober's Lobster Savannah (see page 79). These oysters are delicious and savory.

MUSHROOM CREAM BASE

¼ cup (40 g) shallot, sliced

1 clove garlic, sliced

1 oz (30 ml) dry brandy

1 oz (30 ml) dry sherry

½ oz (14 g) dry porcini mushroom

3 sprigs thyme

2 cups (480 ml) heavy cream

1 tsp salt

OYSTERS

6 oz (168 g) king trumpet mushrooms, sliced

Salt to taste

6 oz (168 g) cooked lobster meat, chopped finely

1 tbsp (3 g) finely chopped chives

1 cup (240 ml) mushroom cream base

12 East Coast oysters, medium size, shucked

Chunk of Parmesan Reggiano for grating

To make the mushroom cream base, sweat the shallot and garlic with a little canola oil until translucent. Add the brandy and sherry. Reduce until almost dry. Add the remaining ingredients and simmer gently 15 to 20 minutes, reducing by one third. Strain sauce and cool.

To make the oysters, preheat the broiler. Sauté the mushrooms in a hot pan until golden and cooked through, seasoning with salt. Cool and chop finely. In a bowl, mix the chopped mushrooms, lobster, chives and cream base. Season with salt if necessary. Arrange the oysters on a sheet pan covered with crumpled foil to hold the shells in place. Heap a spoonful of the mushroom mix on each oyster, covering completely. Grate Parmesan over top. Broil at a medium distance from the heating element until golden and bubbly, about 5 to 6 minutes. Be careful not to broil too quickly or oysters will still be raw underneath. Serve immediately.

KEN ORINGER'S MUSHROOMS SAN SEBASTIAN

SERVES 6

In his own words: "This mushroom recipe was inspired by my travels to San Sebastian, Spain, during mushroom season early in autumn.

My favorite restaurant there is Ganbara. It serves a dish of sautéed mushrooms simply prepared with garlic, parsley and sea salt, drizzled with olive oil and topped with a fresh egg yolk. You mix the yolk into the mushrooms and it creates a creamy umami-bomb of rich, savory flavor.

I travel with Jay, too, as often as I can and of course we talk about food nonstop. He's always interested in learning about new foods. We are fortunate enough each year to cook at the Food & Wine Classic in Aspen, Colorado. Last year Jay and I thought it would be great to re-create those San Sebastian mushrooms. We served them to thousands of people each day at the base of the mountain. We had such a blast that day with this incredible recipe that I thought it'd be a fun one to share for Jay's book."

¼ cup (60 ml) olive oil

½ lb (227 g) fresh chanterelle mushrooms, cleaned

½ lb (227 g) hen of the woods mushrooms, roughly chopped

½ lb (227 g) oyster mushrooms, roughly chopped

½ lb (227 g) shitake mushrooms, quartered

½ lb (227 g) fresh porcini mushrooms, sliced (if not fresh use dried)

½ tsp sea salt

¼ tsp pepper

2 cloves garlic, minced

4 shallots, minced

4 sprigs fresh thyme, picked and chopped

½ cup (120 ml) sherry

1 cup (240 ml) chicken stock

1 tsp soy sauce

1 bunch Italian parsley, roughly chopped

1 bunch chives, finely chopped

3 tbsp (42 g) butter, unsalted

1 tsp fresh-squeezed lemon juice

6 egg yolks

Place a large casserole dish or sauté pan over medium-high heat. When the pan is hot but not smoking, add the olive oil around and swirl around to coat the pan. Add all the mushrooms and stir to coat with oil. Season with salt and pepper. Add the garlic and shallots and cook until the mushrooms are browning and releasing some liquid, about 10 minutes. Add the thyme, stir and cook 5 more minutes.

Deglaze the pan with sherry, first pulling the pan from the heat to avoid a flame. Return to heat and reduce until pan is dry, about 1 minute. Add chicken stock, soy sauce, parsley, chives and butter. Continue cooking until the mushrooms are reduced and nicely glazed. When there is only a little sauce left in the pan, remove from the heat and sprinkle in lemon juice. Spoon the mushrooms into six individual bowls. Drizzle each bowl with olive oil. Form a divot in the center of each bowl of mushrooms with a tablespoon. Place the spoons on top of the divots and place an egg yolk in each spoon. Season yolks with salt and pepper. Serve, instructing guests to mix up the egg yolks into the mushrooms.

CHAPTER 7

New England Country Home

Cooking with friends and cooking for guests are two of the greatest joys in my life. But nothing beats cooking at home for the people I love the most, my wife Janet and our four children, Samira, Mason, Victoria and Miles.

So when Janet and I remodeled a 300-year-old historic home in the Boston suburbs, we had two goals in mind and food was at the center of both plans. One, we wanted to raise as much of our own food as possible right there in our backyard, in a manner that's local and sustainable and that pays tribute to our home's farmhouse roots. And, two, we wanted to prepare that food in a modern kitchen that allowed us to entertain and cook to our heart's desire, while incorporating into the design many of the existing rustic elements of a colonial-era New England home, such as the ancient pinewood timbers, original to the house, that accent our kitchen. It's a little bit of old New England and contemporary design all in one.

We care for 30 to 40 chickens in a large coop a short distance from the back door, providing all of our eggs and much of the poultry we eat. There's plenty of eggs and meat to share with friends and family, too. The birds are mostly heritage breed chickens like Plymouth rocks and Rhode Island reds, both of which have a long connection to New England farming. Raising chickens is a very inexpensive and relatively easy way to take control of your food supply. It's a growing trend and even in a small, urban space you can raise a few birds at any given time, enough to provide eggs for your family each day and plenty of meat, too. There's a good chance your community has an ordinance that allows you to grow chickens.

We also raise a couple of pigs each year. A single 250-pound (113-kg) hog provides nearly 150 pounds (68 kg) of meat which ends up in countless family meals—plenty of fresh pork chops, two racks of ribs and a pair of Boston butts (great for pulled pork) and even our own cured bacons, hams, salamis and prosciutto.

The pork is raised sustainably, locally and humanely right here in our own little neck of the New England woods. The pigs munch on animal feed mixed with food waste from Mike's City Diner and from our own home. Having spent my childhood in a country that never seemed to have enough food, I feel a certain sense of guilt when so much food is thrown away here in many households and restaurants, including my own. The reality is that food waste is a big problem in America and in other developed countries. Some reports say that 40 percent of all food is thrown away. Put most simply, humans raise and then prepare a lot of food that never gets eaten. So using this uneaten food to sustain our livestock helps close that gap and puts food waste back into the food supply.

Raising pigs is not as easy as raising chickens. You definitely need more space, it can cost a lot to feed them and not everyone has access to the food waste we have to supplement feed and cut down the costs of raising the animals. Still, the amount of meat you get from these animals would cost a small fortune in the supermarket, and it's rewarding to maintain some control over the food you serve your family.

When that pork dish calls for parsley, sage, rosemary or thyme we clip the fresh leaves from the plants on our patio herb garden right outside the kitchen door. And in a plot of land beside our house we grow a substantial amount of the produce we eat in season. Plenty of tomatoes, eggplants and root vegetables, to name just a few things we grow. I've grown to enjoy tending to the garden. The actual time spent in the garden is therapeutic in a world otherwise spent glued to our phones and trying to do business. It's also rewarding to care each day for the food that you're going to feed your family.

The kitchen, of course, is where it all comes together. It's the center of our home and where we spend most of our time as a family. And I wanted it to be perfect, the place where we can cook anything we want without the restrictions of a crowded restaurant kitchen. Basically, we wanted our dream kitchen!

The large BlueStar oven gives me room to cook all those turkeys and roasts we need to feed our extended Irish-Lebanese-American family on Thanksgiving and Christmas. We have a gas-powered Marra Forni pizza oven to cook real high-heat pizzas and manakish, plus casseroles and any kind of bread baked right here in our cozy home. I have a guilty pleasure hidden away in our kitchen, too, a large collection of chef's knives. All chefs love their knives. It's the single most important tool of the trade. But I probably go a little overboard. My favorites are the hand-forged, custom-made knives from Bob Kramer Knives of Washington State, made with gorgeous Damascus steel.

We also hang homemade sausages and salamis in the glass-door charcuterie refrigerator, a sort of modern-day larder housing a plump assortment of savory meats. Those ruddy brown smoked sausages lend a very rustic, traditional farmhouse feel to the kitchen. And I spend much of my time at home cooking outdoors, mostly over the grill but also cooking in our outdoor pizza oven. Grilled lamb, fish, chicken and vegetables, many prepared with Middle Eastern style and flavors, are all staples of our family meals.

As for all those vegetables grown in the garden? They enjoy a special place in our kitchen. We can't eat all the vegetables when they're fresh, so we preserve them in mason jars in our pickling pantry. The colors are incredible! The delicate red hue of pickled turnips, deep blackish purple eggplants, bright green pickled tomatoes, the multi-tone orange, yellow and whites of our mixed veggies with carrots, cauliflower, zucchini and onion, the shocking bright red of homemade tomato sauce and even jars of beautiful white labneh cheese floating in a golden bath of olive oil. It's like capturing summer in a jar all year long and you can see all the different colors of the garden through the glass-door cabinets of the pickling cupboard. It adds a mouthwatering vision to the entire room. It also creates a problem: you're instantly hungry once you walk in the kitchen!

The good fortune of a home full of family and great food, here in the safety of small-town New England, always brings me back to my life in the old country, back to Beirut and to the war in the 1970s. It's only in recent years, as a husband and father of four, surrounded by my dream kitchen and the abundance of the New England countryside, that I began to appreciate the struggles my parents Nicolas and Samira faced raising four children of their own in a cramped apartment in the middle of a war zone, with death all around us.

Quite frankly, I never appreciated the pain and anguish they must have suffered as parents, fearful for the lives of their children every morning and every night. I was a little boy. The war did not scare me then. I didn't know any better. But the war scares me today, nearly 40 years later, as I look at my own four children and wonder if I could have been as brave and strong as my parents.

My mother and father coped with the pain and the fright they must have felt and somehow kept our family together. They also found a way to get us to the safety of America and to a brighter future in a country that has allowed me and my sister and my brothers to pursue our dreams. That memory of what my parents did for us fills my heart with love for them, and for my family today and for my good fortune here in the United States. And, to me, the best way to express that love and appreciation is to share great food with friends and family.

GRILLED BUTTERFLIED LEG OF LAMB WITH MINT SALSA VERDE

SERVES 4 TO 6

We eat lamb at home all throughout the year, especially in the winter when we cook it in my pizza oven. But this lamb, grilled outdoors and paired with the gorgeous green salsa verde, is my favorite way to celebrate Easter and the long-awaited warmth and color of spring after a long New England winter.

SALSA VERDE

½ cup (30 g) mint leaves, packed

½ cup (30 g) packed flat parsley leaves

½ cup (34 g) roughly chopped chives

¼ cup (40 g) roughly chopped shallots

1 lemon, zest and juice (at least 2 tbsp [30 ml])

2 tbsp (30 ml) cherry vinegar (or substitute with cider vinegar)

1 tsp crushed red pepper (or more to taste)

2 tsp (10 g) kosher salt

1½ cups (360 ml) extra virgin olive oil

LAMB

1 tsp freshly ground allspice

2 tsp (4 g) ground ginger

2 tsp (4 g) ground cinnamon

4 cloves garlic, minced

1 tbsp (18 g) salt

½ cup (120) oil

1 lemon, zest and juice

5 lb (2.2 kg) leg of lamb, butterflied at the butcher, with fat on it

For the salsa, put all the ingredients in a blender except the oil. Puree 30 to 40 seconds, slowly adding oil until fully emulsified.

For the lamb, whisk together the spices, salt, oil, lemon zest and juice. Put the leg of lamb in a baking dish. Pour the marinade over it and work it into the meat with your hands. Let it rest at least 3 hours or up to 24 hours.

Build a two-zone fire on the grill, with medium to medium-high heat on one side, and no direct heat on second side. Cook each side of the lamb about 15 minutes, making ¼ turn halfway through each side to create crisscross grill marks. Do not burn the lamb. Move off the direct heat to the cool side of grill once you achieve desired color and grill marks. Close the grill top and roast to desired internal temperature, 130 to 135°F (54 to 57°C) for rare, which will happen quickly, or up to 145°F (63°C) for medium, about 5 to 10 minutes. Remove from the heat. Cover loosely in foil and let rest at least 10 minutes. Slice diagonally across the grain, about ½-inch (1.3-cm) thick. Spoon the salsa across the meat, or serve it in a bowl on the side and use it as a dip.

BRAISED CHICKEN WITH 50 CLOVES OF GARLIC

Chicken with garlic is one of my all-time favorite dishes. My mom made it back in Lebanon, and I rediscovered it years later during some return trips to Beirut. I've since made it a part of my personal repertoire, often cooking it for large gatherings, and jazzing it up with 50 cloves of garlic. It sounds great. Looks greats. Tastes great, too! Do you really need 50 cloves of garlic? Not really. But I think all those cloves make for a dramatic name and dramatic flavor. You can use more or less garlic as desired.

4 to 5 lb (1.8 to 2.2 kg) chicken thighs, brined (page 115)

1 tbsp (18 g) salt

1 tbsp (6 g) Aleppo pepper

¼ cup (60 ml) olive oil

50 cloves of garlic (or more!)

½ cup (120 ml) cherry wine

2½ cups (600 ml) chicken stock

½ cup (120 ml) fresh-squeezed lemon juice

1 tsp ground cumin

3 tbsp (9 g) fresh chopped parsley, divided

Optional: 1 tbsp salt + 1 tsp black pepper to taste

Brine chicken at least 4 hours or overnight. Preheat oven to 350°F (176°C). Pat the chicken dry and season well with the salt and Aleppo pepper (or more to taste). Heat the olive oil to medium-hot in a 6- to 8-quart (5- to 7-L) Dutch heavy or heavy pot. Sear the chicken until well browned on both sides, about 4 minutes per side. Cook in batches if needed so as not to overcrowd the pan and cool off the oil. Transfer the chicken to a baking dish and pack together snugly.

Add the garlic to the pot and cook in the remaining oil and chicken scrapings until lightly browned, about 3 to 4 minutes, but do not overcook and burn. Stir the garlic gently while sautéeing to color on all sides. Add the cherry wine and stir with a wooden spoon to deglaze the pot until it boils and all the alcohol is cooked off, about 2 to 3 minutes. Add the stock, lemon juice and cumin. Bring to a boil for 4 to 5 minutes. Shut off the heat. Remove about one-third of the garlic cloves from the pot and set aside. Add 2 tablespoons (6 g) of parsley. Grind with an immersion blender until it becomes a thick sauce, being careful not to splash the very hot liquid on yourself; or mash and whisk the remaining garlic mixture in the pot by hand. Test the flavor and season with salt and black pepper to taste if desired. Pour the ground garlic juice all over the chicken in the baking dish. Put the garlic cloves that were set aside on top of the chicken. Bake for 40 to 45 minutes. Garnish with the remaining parsley and optional salt and pepper. Serve family style on the table.

MOROCCAN-STYLE HARISSA SAUCE

Harissa is a spicy chili paste common in Morocco and in other North African countries. It's incredibly versatile and I love to use it as many ways as possible, as a marinade for meat, for roasting vegetables, as a dip on its own or even as an interesting condiment for burgers and dogs in your backyard barbecue. I also use it on my Manakish (see page 58). But mostly I love to use harissa to marinate meats. Whip up a batch of harissa sauce and refrigerate it until you're ready to add a spicy splash of ethnic flavor to whatever you might be cooking.

3 oz (84 g) dried guajillo chiles, stemmed and seeded

1 tsp caraway seeds

1 tsp coriander seeds

2 tsp (4 g) cumin seeds

2 tsp (10 g) kosher salt

8 cloves garlic

1 cup (240 ml) extra virgin olive oil

Juice of 3 lemons

¾ cup (180 ml) apple cider vinegar

Put the chiles into a medium bowl, cover with boiling water and let sit until softened, about 20 minutes. Heat the caraway, coriander and cumin in a dry skillet over medium heat. Toast the spices, swirling the skillet constantly, until very fragrant, for just a couple minutes, then transfer spices to a grinder. Grind to a fine powder.

Drain the chiles and transfer to a food processor with the ground spices, salt, garlic, olive oil, lemon juice and vinegar. Puree, stopping occasionally to scrape down the sides of the bowl, until smooth, about 2 minutes.

HARISSA-ROASTED CAULIFLOWER

SERVES 4 TO 6 AS SIDE DISH

Cauliflower is delicious but looks a little bland. Roasting cauliflower in harissa sauce instantly solves that problem. Harissa turns the cauliflower all different shades of rich reds and browns in the oven, adding an incredible splash of eye-catching, mouthwatering color to this very simple vegetable dish. Even your kids will want to eat cauliflower when they see it smothered in gorgeous roasted harissa.

1 head of cauliflower, cut into bit-sized florets

1½ cups (360 ml) Moroccan-Style Harissa Sauce (page 160)

1 tbsp (15 ml) olive oil

2 tbsp (2 g) chopped fresh cilantro

Preheat the oven to 450°F (232°C). Mix the florets well by hand with the harissa in a large bowl, so that the sauce is distributed well among all the cauliflower. The florets should be coated with sauce, but not soaking in it. Drizzle a sheet pan with olive oil. Spread the coated florets evenly across the pan. Bake for about 40 minutes, so that the sauce is dried and pops with a deep, bright reddish-brown color. Transfer to serving bowl. Garnish with cilantro.

Harissa is a spicy Moroccan chili paste you can make easily at home.

Pour the harissa over the cauliflower florets, then mix by hand.

The cauliflower comes out of the oven with beautiful, rich red and brown colors.

HARISSA-MARINATED CORNISH GAME HEN

SERVES 4

We raise plenty of chickens in the backyard for both eggs and meat. A marinade bath of harissa and a hot grill are all you need to turn a simple game hen or small chicken into a beautiful and delicious family meal.

1 whole game hen or small chicken, about 1½ lb (681 g)

2½ cups (590 ml) Moroccan-Style Harissa Sauce (page 160), divided

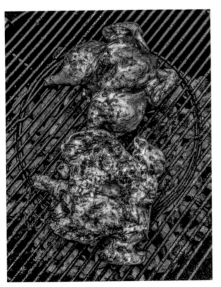

Butterfly the bird: Place the game hen on a cutting board breast-side-down. Working from the cavity opening up to the neck, cut down each side of the back bone with a kitchen scissors and discard the backbone. Open the bird, skin side up, and press down with heel of your hand on top of each breast and on the legs to flatten. Place the bird splayed open in an 8 × 8 inch (20 × 20 cm) baking dish and set aside. Pour harissa sauce over the chicken, reserving about 2 ounces (60 ml) for brushing the chicken while grilling. Marinate in the refrigerator at least 4 hours or overnight.

Heat the grill to medium high. Place the chicken on the grill, skin side up, cover and cook about 20 minutes, brushing the chicken every few minutes with the reserved sauce.

Flip the chicken and cook until the skin is marked with char and the meat is cooked through, about 10 more minutes. Give the chicken a quarter turn after about 5 minutes to create those attractive patchwork grill marks. The chicken is done if juices run clear when thigh is pierced. Transfer the chicken to a platter and let it rest for a few minutes. Serve with hummus, tabouli and/or grilled pita bread.

GRILLED SESAME- AND SUMAC-CRUSTED TUNA WITH SOY VINAIGRETTE

Sesame and sumac are two of my favorite spices, each used in various recipes throughout this book. The sesame seeds give the tuna steaks some delicious crunchy texture, while the sumac adds that incredible lemon tartness that pairs so perfectly with rich, flavorful, high-quality tuna.

VINAIGRETTE

1½-inch (4-cm) thick slice of medium-sized red onion

Dash of olive oil

2 tbsp (30 ml) lemon juice

1 tbsp (15 ml) soy sauce

½ cup (120 ml) extra virgin olive oil

1 tsp sumac

1 tsp kosher salt or sea salt

1 tbsp (10 g) finely chopped shallot

1 clove garlic, mashed

TUNA STEAK

1 tbsp (15 ml) olive oil

2 tbsp (12 g) dried sumac

1 tbsp (15 g) sesame seeds

2 (6-oz [168-g]) tuna steaks, about 1¼-inch (3-cm) thick each

For the dressing, heat the grill to high. Lightly coat the onion slice with a dash of olive oil. Char the onion on the grill until blackened but not cooked through, about 4 to 5 minutes per side. Let the onion cool to room temperature. Chop finely. Whisk together the lemon juice, soy sauce, extra virgin olive oil, sumac, salt, shallot and garlic with about 1 tablespoon (10 g) of blackened chopped onion.

To grill the tuna, pour the olive oil in a flat dish. Mix together the sumac and sesame in a separate flat dish. Dip the tuna in oil and spread the oil around with your fingers until the entire steak is covered. Dry your fingers and hands of oil. Then dip the oiled steak in the sumac-sesame mixture. Heat the grill to high. Grill the tuna steak about 1 minute per side (for rare). Let the tuna cool first to room temperature, about 5 to 10 minutes. Drizzle with soy vinaigrette.

GRILLED SWORDFISH IN CHARRED GRAPE LEAVES

SERVES 2

The pickled grape leaves in this dish make an ideal pocket in which to steam your swordfish to delicious perfection on the grill. This dish is very simple, but very elegant and flavorful and can make you look like a master of the backyard grill.

2 (6-oz [168-g]) swordfish steaks

1 tsp kosher salt

1 tsp fresh ground black pepper

Juice of two lemon wedges

8 to 10 pickled grape leaves

Olive oil

2 lemon quarters

2 pinches ground sumac

Heat the grill to hot. Sprinkle the swordfish steaks on both sides with salt and pepper. Layer 5 grape leaves so they're overlapping. Place a steak in the center of the leaves. Squeeze the juice of one lemon wedge over each steak. Roll up the leaves over the short ends of the steak, and then roll up one side of the leaves over long end of the steak. Flip the steak over lengthwise and wrap tightly with the remaining overlapping leaves. Repeat with the second steak. Grape leaves will keep the steak moist and add smoky flavor.

Brush the leaves lightly with olive oil. Place the wrapped swordfish on a hot grill, cooking about 4 to 5 minutes per side, being careful not to overcook.

Remove the swordfish from the grill and let rest 2 to 3 minutes, with the grape leaf wrapper still around the steaks. Grill the lemon quarters until lightly charred. Unwrap the grape leaves carefully and plate the swordfish. Drizzle with olive oil and sprinkle with sumac. Garnish with grilled lemon quarters.

IMAM BAYILDI

Imam bayildi is a stuffed or grilled eggplant dish common in the Mediterranean world, but originating in Turkey. The name, translated from Turkish, means "the Imam fainted." It's so good that, according to legend, it caused a hungry imam to faint with joy. I don't know if you'll faint. But you will find it a delicious way to prepare all those garden herbs and vegetables in your own backyard.

2 medium eggplants, cut into ½-inch (1.3-cm) thick slices

2 to 3 tbsp (15 to 30 g) kosher salt

1 large red onion, cut into ½-inch (1.3-cm) thick slices

¼ cup (60 ml) olive oil, divided

1½ lb (681 g) fresh garden tomatoes, halved

3 garlic cloves, finely chopped

½ cup (30 g) roughly chopped flat parsley

2 tbsp (10 g) finely chopped fresh basil

2 tbsp (30 ml) balsamic vinegar

2 tbsp (17 g) capers, drained

Kosher salt and pepper to taste

Place the eggplant slices in a colander and sprinkle generously with salt. Let sit about 1 hour. Before using, rinse the salt off the eggplant and pat dry.

Preheat a gas grill to high, or build a hot charcoal fire. Brush both sides of the eggplant and onion slices with some of the olive oil. Place the eggplant, onion and tomatoes on the hot grill. You will probably have to work in batches, so as to not overcrowd the grill.

Grill the eggplant about 7 to 8 minutes per side. The eggplant is ready when soft. Grill the onions until charred, about 4 minutes per side. Grill the tomatoes on each side until slightly charred and cooked all the way through. Peel the skin from the tomatoes. The skin should come off easily when cooked through. Move the eggplant, onion and tomatoes to a cutting board and give them a rough chop. Transfer to large bowl and mix with all remaining ingredients including the remaining olive oil. Refrigerate overnight. Eat cold or at room temperature as a healthy midday snack or as a side to favorite grilled meats.

BATINJAN MASHWI
(SMOKY GRILLED EGGPLANT AND TOMATO)

I love eggplant and always have and grow a ton of them in my garden each year. They look beautiful and taste great, too. They're a sure sign of the bounty of summer. It doesn't take a lot to prepare great eggplant, either. I simply throw one on the grill—preferably over a wood fire—with a big, fat red fresh-off-the-vine tomato. Grill both until they're soft, splash with a little lemon sauce, salt and some herbs and, voilá! You have a perfect summertime dish you can serve as a side with just about any kind of grilled meat.

3 tbsp (60 ml) extra virgin olive oil

1 tbsp (15 ml) lemon juice

⅛ tsp crushed red pepper flakes

2 cloves garlic, minced

Dash of salt and pepper to taste

1 large whole eggplant

1 large red tomato

Sprinkle of kosher salt

Sprinkle of chopped parsley

Whisk together olive oil, lemon juice, red pepper flakes, minced garlic and dash of salt and pepper in a small bowl. Set aside or refrigerate until ready to cook eggplant.

Heat the grill to high. Poke about 10 small holes around the eggplant with the tip of a knife, which will help release steam as the eggplant cooks. Place the eggplant and the tomato on the grill at the same time. Cook the tomato, stem side down, about 5 minutes. Then flip, placing bottom side down, and cook additional 10 minutes. The tomato will be nicely charred when done. Lay the eggplant on its side and cook about 12 minutes. Then rotate the eggplant 180 degrees and cook the other side about another 12 minutes. The eggplant is done when the skin is very thin and papery and the flesh inside is very, very soft to the touch. Cook longer if eggplant is not very soft. It will appear to lose its shape, almost like a deflated American football, when ready.

Plate and slit the eggplant from top to bottom to butterfly and open it up. Mash up the tomato on top of the eggplant. Use a spoon to separate the meat of the eggplant from the skin. Pour sauce over the meat and garnish with kosher salt and chopped parsley.

MOUSSAKA CASSEROLE WITH BÉCHAMEL SAUCE

SERVES 6 TO 8

Moussaka is another dish closely associated with Turkey, but available throughout the Arab world, too. My mother made a version of moussaka that was, in the Arab tradition, typically served cold. My moussaka is very rich and savory and topped with a creamy béchamel, one of the "mother sauces" of French cuisine that influenced the food and culture of Lebanon. My moussaka is best served hot. But you could eat it at room temperature or even cold, too, if you wanted.

BÉCHAMEL SAUCE

4 tbsp (56 g) unsalted butter

7 tbsp (55 g) all-purpose flour

3½ cups (830 ml) whole milk, hot but not scalded or boiling

1 cup (112 g) high-quality imported provolone cheese, shredded

Salt and pepper to taste

CASSEROLE

1 large potato

2 large eggplants

1 tbsp (15 ml) olive oil plus more for brushing eggplant

1 lb (454 g) lean ground beef

1 large yellow onion

2 garlic cloves, crushed

3 tbsp (48 g) tomato paste

½ cup (120 ml) beef or chicken stock

1½ tsp (5 g) cinnamon

½ tsp nutmeg

Salt to taste

To make the sauce, melt the butter over medium heat in a sauté pan. Add the flour slowly and whisk constantly to avoid burning, cooking for about 1 minute. Add 1 cup (240 ml) of milk and whisk. Then add the remaining milk in portions. Whisk until smooth, about 5 minutes or until the sauce thickens. Remove from the heat. Whisk in the cheese. Add salt and pepper.

Preheat the oven to 350°F (176°C). Peel the potato, slice to ¼-inch (6-mm) thick and boil gently until soft but not mushy, about 15 minutes. Peel most of the skin off the eggplants, but leave some thin strips behind, then slice to ½-inch (12-mm) thick. Brush eggplant slices with olive oil on both sides. Place in a single layer on a baking sheet. Bake 20 to 25 minutes, or until eggplant is browned and softened. Remove from the oven and let cool.

Heat the oil in a skillet over medium heat. Brown the ground beef and break apart, until it's just about to turn brown. Add onion and garlic and cook about 6 more minutes until onion is softened and most of the grease cooks away. If there is too much oil, just pour off most of it. Add remaining ingredients, mix up very well and bring to a boil. Reduce heat and simmer until mixture is dried.

Grease a 9 × 13 inch (23 × 33 cm) casserole pan very lightly. Add half the eggplant. Layer the potato over the eggplant, then add the ground beef mixture, then top with a second layer of eggplant. Make sure the layers are even and level. Pour béchamel over the top ensuring it fills in the nooks and crannies. Bake 40 to 45 minutes, or until golden brown. If not browned after 45 minutes, put under broiler briefly to brown the top.

THE ART OF "READING" A COFFEE CUP

Reading coffee cups is a Middle Eastern folk tradition and a form of fortune telling, usually practiced by women around the dinner table during and after dessert. There's actually a scientific name for reading coffee cups called tasseography.

My mom loved reading coffee cups and it's one of my favorite memories of her from our time in the old country and even here in Boston. I can still picture my dad and mom leisurely sipping coffee together each morning. But my favorite memory may be that of my mom sitting underneath the grapevine next to our driveway in Roslindale on beautiful summer nights, holding court and reading coffee cup fortunes for all our Lebanese neighbors. I smile everytime I think about it.

Here's how it works. Drinking coffee in Lebanon and in other countries in that part of the world is a lot different than drinking coffee in the United States. First of all, drinking coffee is a slow and leisurely communal activity. Coffee is not something you grab by yourself at the local take-out coffee shop to pound down on the way into work. And second, you steep the coffee right over the ground beans without filtering out the grinds.

The grounds in Arab coffee are very fine, and they settle into a thick, muddy sludge in the bottom of the coffee pot and also in the bottom of your coffee cup. When you're done drinking you tip the cup upside down and all the coffee grounds pour out and they leave behind a lacework of residue around the cup. Coffee readers like my mom interpret these lines and swirls to read your fortune.

Is there any truth to it? I don't know. I'm not sure even my mom believed in it. Reading fortunes was a sin in our religion and my mom would always say, "God forgive me" just before reaching for the next cup and reading another fortune.

But it was all in good fun around family and friends and we always had a great time laughing over the next fortune, while enjoying some delicious Middle Eastern desserts.

NAMOURA (SEMOLINA COCONUT CAKE)

We grew up with this dessert around the holidays and it was always one of my favorites, with the soft semolina cake, almost like a sponge cake, topped with an almond for texture and doused in a delicious simple syrup that melts into the cake. Perfect with coffee!

SIMPLE SYRUP

½ cup (100 g) sugar

½ cup (120 ml) water

½ tsp freshly grated lemon zest

1 tsp lemon juice

1 tsp orange blossom water

CAKE

20 whole almonds

2 cups (334 g) No. 1 or No. 2 fine semolina

½ cup (100 g) sugar

1 cup (93 g) shredded coconut

¼ tsp baking soda

½ tsp baking powder

1 cup (240 ml) whole-milk yogurt

8 tbsp (112 ml) melted butter

To make the simple syrup, put the sugar, water and lemon zest in a small sauce pan. Bring to a boil over high heat, whisking occasionally. Reduce heat to gentle boil for 2 to 3 minutes. Remove from heat. Whisk in lemon juice and blossom water. Let cool to room temperature.

To make the cake, begin by blanching the almonds by placing them in boiling water. Remove immediately from the heat and let sit in the hot water for 20 minutes. Drain the almonds. The skins should now be easy to remove by squeezing the almonds with your fingers. Set the almonds aside.

Preheat the oven to 400°F (204°C). Combine the semolina, sugar, coconut, baking soda and baking powder in a bowl and whisk together well. Add yogurt and melted butter. Mix well with hands until you have a firm batter. Grease a 9 × 13 inch (23 × 33 cm) brownie pan with butter. Spread the batter evenly across the pan. Smooth the top of the batter with a wet hand or the back of a wet tablespoon. The batter should be both even and very smooth.

Lightly score the cake into 20 individual squares about 2 inches (5 cm) each. Press an almond into each square so that the almond is even with the top of the batter. Bake 30 minutes or until the top is golden brown. Remove the cake from the oven. Pour the cool syrup over the baked cake while the cake is still hot, so that it will absorb the syrup. Let cool and serve at room temperature.

KATAIFI COOKIE SANDWICHES WITH MASCARPONE CREAM

Kataifi is a shredded pastry cookie common in Lebanon, but that I had never tasted until I went back to Beirut as an adult. My own little twist is to turn them into a sort of Lebanese sandwich cookie, filled with sweetened mascarpone cream.

CREAM

½ cup (60 g) mascarpone cheese

½ cup (120 ml) heavy cream

3 tbsp (38 g) sugar

½ tsp vanilla extract

½ tsp orange blossom water

COOKIE

8 oz (224 g) shredded kataifi dough

8 tbsp (112 ml) melted butter

2 tbsp (25 g) sugar

2 tbsp (15 g) pistachios, shelled and medium chopped

To make the cream, put the mascarpone, cream, sugar, vanilla and orange blossom water in a bowl and blend with a hand mixer on low speed. Turn the mixer to high as all the ingredients blend together. Mix until peaks form, anywhere from 3 to 5 minutes. Make sure you move the mixer around the bowl to blend all of the cream evenly. Cover the bowl with plastic wrap and refrigerate at least 4 hours or overnight.

For the cookies, preheat the oven to 400°F (204°C). Chop the strings of kataifi dough into lengths of about ¼ inch (6 mm). Place the dough and melted butter in a bowl and mix very well with your hands. Gently untangle and loosen the strings of dough as much as possible while tossing. The melted butter will help the entangled strings pull apart. Add the sugar and pistachios and, using a gentle tossing motion, mix in very well with your hands. The pistachios should be evenly mixed throughout the dough and not stuck on the bottom of the bowl.

Now, find a cookie cutter that's just large enough to fit around a standard soup can, about 2¾ inches (7 cm) in diameter. Lay the cookie cutter on a baking sheet and place about 1½ to 2 tablespoons (20 to 30 ml) of dough in the bottom of the cookie cutter. Then, using the soup can as a press, insert the can into the cookie cutter and press down firmly but gently. The resulting cookie should be about ¼-inch (6-mm) thick. Repeat the process until all the dough has been used, making sure to plan ahead and evenly space the dough on the baking sheet before baking, as the cookie dough is hard to move. You should end up with 20 to 24 individual cookies.

If the dough sticks to the soup can, simply spray the can with some cooking spray. Bake in the middle rack of your oven, about 10 to 15 minutes until golden brown, spinning the baking sheet after about 7 minutes. Keep a close eye on the cookies, as they are very delicate. They will turn golden brown quickly and will burn if left in the oven too long.

Let cookies cool at least 2 hours or overnight. The cookies freeze well. When ready to serve, place 1 tablespoon (15 ml) of cream each on half the cookies. Then top with the remaining cookies.

KAAK BITAMER (LEBANESE DATE COOKIES)

When I was a kid my mom made these cookies around the holidays, especially at Easter. The date filling is only slightly sweet but still delicious, with an amazing soft and chewy texture. Back in Lebanon dates were cheaper than other types of cookie fillings like pistachios or walnuts. So we ate these cookies all the time. I still make them today for holiday parties, each cookie prepared meticulously by hand. They're worth every second.

FILLING

12-14 oz (336–392 g) dried unsweetened dates, pitted

1½ tsp (3 g) cinnamon

½ tsp nutmeg

2 tbsp (28 g) unsalted butter, melted

DOUGH

2 cups (334 g) fine semolina

½ cup (63 g) all-purpose flour

⅓ cup (66 g) sugar

10 tbsp (140 g) unsalted butter, melted

1½ tbsp (23 ml) orange blossom water

¼ cup (60 ml) whole milk

¼ tsp quick-rise yeast

Confectioner's sugar

To make the filling, blend the dates, cinnamon and nutmeg in a food processor until mostly smooth, but still with some granular texture. The texture really adds to the quality of the cookie. Place the date and spice mixture in bowl and mix in the melted butter very well by hand. The dates don't really absorb the liquid of the butter like flour does. So you'll probably have to keep folding in and squeezing the mixture together by hand until everything is mixed together well and there are no more traces of butter left in the bowl. Form into a log and cover with plastic wrap until ready to make cookies.

Place the semolina, flour and sugar in a medium-sized bowl and whisk together well. Add the melted butter and mix with your hands and work together well. Add the blossom water, milk and yeast and work into a stiff dough, again using your hands. It should have the texture and look of Play-Doh. Form into a ball and cover with plastic wrap. Refrigerate for 30 to 45 minutes, just long enough to chill through and stiffen the dough slightly. If dough turns too stiff, warm slightly at room temperature. Measure out 1 ounce (28 g) of dough and ½ ounce (14 g) of date filling for each cookie and, using slightly wet hands, form both the dough and the filling into balls. Form all of the dough and filling into balls before forming the cookies. At this point, preheat the oven to 400°F (204°C).

Again using slightly wet hands, gently work each ball of dough by pressing your thumbs into the middle and spreading out the edges with your fingers to form a cavity in the middle, almost like the shape of an umbrella hood. Place a ball of date filling in the cavity and then gently manipulate the edges of the dough down to completely cover the filling. Roll the entire thing into a ball with your hands. At this point, you can gently flatten each ball into a round cookie of about 2 to 2½ inches (5 to 6 cm) wide and about ⅓ to ½ inch (5 to 10 mm) thick.

Or, if you prefer, use a medium-sized Lebanese cookie mold (called a mámoul mold), which will give the cookie its traditional festive design. Spray the mold lightly with cooking spray. Gently press the dough into the mold until it's flattened evenly. Then flip the mold over and slam the end on the table and the formed cookie dough will pop out.

Place the dough on a flat cookie sheet and bake 20 to 25 minutes or until lightly browned. Sprinkle with confectioner's sugar.

BOOZA (PISTACHIO CARDAMOM ICE CREAM)

Booza is a form of ice cream popular in certain parts of the Arab world, especially around Lebanon, and made with the gum of the mastic tree, a relative of the pistachio. The mastic gum helps keep the ice cream from melting so quickly, which is important in hot climates.

Kids in Lebanon don't eat ice cream the way kids do here in America. We might have eaten booza once or twice a year. So this ice cream was very special to me. I loved it as a boy in Beirut and looked forward eagerly to the one or two times a year when we might have some. It felt like waking up on Christmas anytime we got to enjoy it.

1 cup (200 g) sugar

4 cups (950 ml) whole milk, divided

2 cups (480 ml) heavy whipping cream

½ cup (64 g) cornstarch

½ tsp orange blossom water

1 tsp vanilla extract

½ tsp ground cardamom

¼ tsp ground mastic gum

¾ cup (93 g) shelled unsalted pistachios, roughly chopped

In a medium-heavy sauce pan, add sugar, 3 cups (710 ml) of the milk and all the heavy cream. Bring to a simmer over medium-low heat. Meanwhile, whisk very well the remaining 1 cup (140 ml) of milk with cornstarch, blossom water, vanilla, cardamom and mastic gum. Pour the cornstarch mixture into the simmering pot of milk and cream. Increase the heat and bring the mixture to a gentle, controlled boil for 1 minute, stirring constantly so as not to burn the milk. Pour the mixture into a stainless steel bowl and let cool to room temperature, stirring occasionally. Cover the bowl tightly with plastic wrap and refrigerate at least 4 hours or overnight. Freeze in an ice cream machine, according to directions on the machine. If the ice cream machine is too small, make ice cream in separate batches. When the ice cream is still spinning and almost done, gently pour in the pistachios. Scoop the ice cream into a shallow container. Cover, if desired, and freeze at least 4 hours.

ACKNOWLEDGMENTS

A cookbook doesn't come together overnight or by itself. In my case, this book took a lot of time, teamwork and inspiration from so many different people.

I drew my earliest inspiration from my older brothers Elias and Michael and my older sister Micheline, who encouraged me with their words through the years but mostly with their actions. Each is a great success in their various careers, each a champion of the American Dream that inspired our parents to leave behind their lives in Lebanon back in 1978. Elias, Michael and Micheline in turn inspired me to chase my dreams. Our mom is very proud of all of them. I know my late dad is, too.

Jamie Bissonnette and Ken Oringer, meanwhile, are two of the best chefs in the nation. The crowds at their restaurants say it all. It was Jamie who first encouraged me to write a cookbook. He told me that more people need to know about my food and encouraged me to put pen to paper and share my recipes. And it was Ken who reignited my love of cooking. They have both taught me so much.

My friend and co-author Kerry J. Byrne is not only one of the nation's best food writers, but also one its best football writers. A very unique talent. When it came time to write this book, Kerry was the only person I wanted to work with. I'm so glad I made that decision. It was Kerry who saw what he called the "dramatic story line" and the "culinary journey" of my life. He turned this book into something more than just a collection of recipes. He made this book a very personal story for me and my family and hopefully a book you enjoy, too.

This book would certainly not be possible without William Kiester, Marissa Giambelluca and the entire team at Page Street Publishing. They first and foremost gave a shot to a first-time author, then took another chance when we presented to them a cookbook concept that also serves as a personal memoir. Thank you for your support and guidance throughout the process.

Of course, I have to thank the people of Boston, and specifically our neighbors in the South End, not to mention every guest who has ever walked through the door of Mike's City Diner over the years. You embraced Mike's and made this business the success that it is today. Sure, we cook and serve the food and do the best job we can every single day. But it's our guests who make Mike's feel special—who make it feel like a cozy small-town neighborhood eatery right here in the heart of the big city. Thank you for your loyal support. This book was inspired by every single person who has ever enjoyed our food.

BEIRUT TO BOSTON: A COOKBOOK

I should mention that the guests at Mike's City Diner love the restaurant not only for its food, but because we have the best team in the business. Our crew in the kitchen consistently delivers great meals, usually in a very fast-paced environment. It's hard work and they do it with great skill. And our serving staff creates a warm, inviting environment for every visitor, the kind of service that makes our food taste better and encourages people to visit us again. Thank you Barbara Benatuil, who manages Mike's City Diner day to day, and to everyone who works here and who helps make Mike's the wonderful institution it's become for the people of Boston and for visitors from far and wide.

Finally, and most importantly, I have to thank my children, Samira, Mason, Victoria and Miles, and my wife Janet. My beautiful, talented children are the reason I was put on this earth. They make me proud every day and I hope I do the same for them. I hope this book helps them understand a little bit more about their old man and about the history of our family.

Of course, none of this, my career, my family, this cookbook, would have been possible without Janet. She has stood by me every step of the way. She believed in me, and in us, from the time we were just kids. She was my friend and confidante and inspiration when times were tough and the future uncertain. When it came time to write this book, she was my sounding board, proofreader and taste tester. This book tells the story of my culinary journey. Janet has been my beautiful travel partner during that journey for more than 20 years.

Janet, my life changed the day you walked through the doors of Temptations Café in Brookline all those years ago. None of this would be possible without you. Thank you and I love you.

ABOUT THE AUTHORS

JAY HAJJ is the chef and owner of Mike's City Diner, a beloved casual-dining destination in Boston's beautiful South End neighborhood proclaimed as one of the nation's best diners. Jay and his carefully perfected versions of classic American diner cuisine have been featured numerous times on Food Network programs such as *Diners, Drive-Ins, and Dives*, *Guy's Big Bite* and *Guy's Grocery Games*. He is also a landlord and partner behind many of the city's most prominent eateries, including Yvonne's, the critically acclaimed modern "supper club" in downtown Boston's culinary landmark Locke-Ober building. Jay was born in Beirut in 1970, then fled to America with his family to escape the violence of the Lebanese Civil War, arriving in Boston's working-class Roslindale neighborhood in 1978. Jay opened his first eatery, the Middle Eastern–flavored Temptations Café, at age 20, before taking over Mike's City Diner in 1996. Today, he lives with his wife Janet, their four children and two dogs in a historic 18th-century farmhouse outside Boston, where he raises chickens and pigs and tends to his herb and vegetable gardens, while traveling to cooking events around the globe.

KERRY J. BYRNE is a longtime food writer for the *Boston Herald*, has covered the American craft beer scene since 1993 and was twice named North American Beer Writer of the Year at the Great American Beer Festival. His food and drinks writing has appeared in *Esquire*, *Yankee Magazine*, *Boston Magazine* and Condé Nast publications. Kerry is also the founder of FootballNation.com and ColdHardFootballFacts.com, where he pioneered the statistical analysis of professional football. He is a former NFL columnist for SportsIllustrated.com and a frequent commentator on the NFL Network and sports radio programs around the country. Kerry lives in Quincy, Massachusetts and today runs KJB Trending Hospitality, a boutique marketing, public relations and consulting company.

INDEX